PROPHECY FOR ANYONE

PROPHECY FOR ANYONE

Stirring the Waters of Christian Prophecy

JENNY CAMPBELL

Rehoboth Media
Ashill • 2017

Published by Rehoboth Media

The Well Christian Centre
Swaffham Road,
Ashill, Norfolk
IP25 7BT

www.fountainnetwork.org

ISBN 978-0-9574813-8-1

CONTENTS

INTRODUCTION

The reason for writing this book is to stir the waters of Christian prophecy, to stimulate discussion in church groups, leadership teams, even in the market place. But it is also written to ramp up prophecy to provoke positive and life-changing *action*. What is the bottom line, the underlying question? Will the Church continue to frown upon prophecy, handling it as a hot potato, or will it begin to engage wholeheartedly with this gift of God's grace? Not with unwilling exasperation, as for a perverse toddler, but with gratitude embracing its beauty and strength.

It is every Christian's birthright to hear the Lord, to know the path. We are entitled to hear that voice behind us: 'This is the way; walk in it' (Isa. 30:21). As leaders, we need prophetic vision to hear and see God and people expect godly visionary leadership.

As I observe our times and our helplessness very often in knowing what to do in them (I write this on the morning after the Manchester Arena suicide bombing where an eight-year old was among the twenty-two dead and fifty-nine wounded), I contemplate in a spirit of prayerful urgency this wonderful and powerful gift.

In the run-up to 2020, the world rocks ever more dangerously on the turbulent tides of the terror of Islamic State violence, the unpredictable face of nationalism and state protectionism, dictatorships, an utterly overwhelming refugee crisis in the wake of terrible wars, and the shocking, age-old famines and natural disasters. Are these issues simply old hat, nothing new under the sun, the evil that we do under the sun? What, in heaven's name, is the Church to say? What on earth is the Church to do? And how shall Christians be and act when the rest of planet earth airily dismisses us as pathetic, useless and irrelevant? Can the Church turn the tide of apathy? Can the Church be outspoken for truth? Can the people of God be audacious, fearless, caring and courageous?

Two weeks after that diabolic Manchester tragedy, an emotional Justin Bieber, the young hitmaker, delivered a powerful message at a tribute concert: 'God is good in the midst of the evil. God is good in the midst of the darkness. He loves you.' Hey, you shout out, the gospel is much more than words, words, and yet more words. What rights has pious praying Peter in war-torn devastations tortured by cries for justice and humanitarian aid, where multitudes clamour for water and food?

During a recent catastrophic calamity, where raging forest fires devoured the town of Knysna, South Africa, an online columnist raged against praying Christians who presumed that their god had not caused the desolation and was not evil. And while the philosophic speculations run amok, we do our best but, quite frankly, are overwhelmed by the bottomless pit of human need. For most of us that is the point of disconnect. Our own lives, with their desires and problems, absorb and engulf us. Please don't give us the world's troubles as well! We stop our ears to the cacophony, immunised to pain by its sheer volume.

Can prophecy help me, just an ordinary person, to hear the Lord? This book is driven by a sure and certain faith that the gift of prophecy can indeed tell us who we are and who God is, what to do and how to do it. It has the capacity to unlock doors for strategic plans for every disciple of Jesus from the pope, archbishop or minister, in council, synod, service of worship, mission outreach, work of mercy or prayer meeting.

Prophecy is a key to an energised Church in every part of its multifaceted life. And beyond Church there is the amazing possibility that the word of God could range freely in a world consumed by human solutions in state departments and corridors of power, on the sports fields and celebrity platforms, in schools and universities, in business, in the arts and entertainment industries.

Ha! Leaders cry out: there's the rub and the nub of the trouble. Prophets on the loose, upending the status quo, running wild, divisive and disruptive, clearly out of control—not on my watch! On whose shoulders then the burden of the night thief? For while we sleep, the New Age guru muscles in to steal, weighing in with counterfeit gold: Eastern meditation techniques, horoscope, dream catcher, fairies, angels. Surfeited and drowsy the flock, beguiled and tantalised by bewitching notions of the sweet by-and-by and what is to come, are led astray by another voice.

On the other hand, the sane and sensible vigorously object: I listen to the weather prophet, the economic forecaster, the political predictor. Surely there's nothing wrong with good common sense?

Also (said with a knowing nod), the Church already has the mind of Christ and this is found supremely in Scripture, isn't that so? Why do we need anything extra? And of course, the Bible is everything, and no prophecy may counter or contradict its message. However, we need God's messages for specific situations so that we may understand the times and what to do in them. That's all very well, you may respond, but can we trust implicitly that this message is truly given by God? Do we know that it is trustworthy and not from some other dodgy source? There are many voices out there. How can we tell which one is the Lord's?

This book tackles some of these questions in six short chapters. The first three are theoretical. Chapter 1 sets the scene for Christian prophecy by seeing what's trending as the world peers into the future. Chapter 2 tests the source by spotting three signposts to a true word from God, i.e. scripture, Jesus Christ and the Holy Spirit. Chapter 3 discusses strengthening prophetic vision by examining three streams in the worldwide church.

Having been theoretical, we must then be pragmatic and fit together three practical pieces in the puzzle. Chapter 4 looks at freeing up prophecy by imitating the practices of the New Testament Church and investing in prophetic leadership by means of the fivefold ministry (Eph 4:7-11). Chapter 5 gets down to fast-tracking prophecy by doing away with prophetic professionalism, the nuts and bolts of words and pictures, visions and dreams for anyone. Chapter 6 makes a stab at the thorny matter of prophetic flakiness by commending open communication in prophecies, prophets, and leaders, and seeing life-transforming prophetic communities of faith.

Each chapter is followed by questions for further discussion in leadership teams, home groups and among friends, in the hope of stimulating action in the field of prophecy for anyone: that leaders might inspire and teach the gift and that prophecy might truly be the coupling mechanism which fixes head to body, Jesus Christ to his Church, for 'We have the mind of Christ' (1 Cor. 2:16).

1

SEEING THE TIMES: FUTURE FIRST

In C.S. Lewis' book *The Screwtape Letters*, Screwtape, a senior devil tries to teach his nephew Wormwood, a very junior devil, the art of temptation. The best way to tempt humans, instructs Screwtape, is to coax them away from the present so that they become obsessed by the future, by visions of heaven or hell on earth. Muddle the present and the future and we will produce a race of people who are never happy or kind *now*. This canny ploy works! By living in a never-never world we settle for a permanent state of anxiety. We are precariously poised in the pressure of the present, yet restlessly fixated with the future. We crystal-gaze, mesmerised by the future tense, even though we think we are grounded, hard-nosed realists.

Our forecasting is crazily haphazard. There are those of us, probably the majority, who read the future entirely without religion or anything vaguely 'spiritual'. These are the non-religious or secular forecasters. But then there are those who claim a path of paranormal enlightenment where illumination is given not from a human source, but also not from God. These predict the future by using codes and symbols. Hearing voices.

Energies. In practice, how do these two trends work?

EXAMINING TRENDS

Firstly, we see what's trending in non-religious projections. In our age of 24/7 news desks on phones, television, radios, YouTube, Twitter, Facebook, Instagram, and other social networks, we are bombarded incessantly with the latest horrifying global happening. We are fed daily bread which sends us into a dizzy spin. Reports of earthquakes, economic collapse, hurricanes, war, storms, fires, shipwrecks, airplane casualties, volcanoes, murders and urban terrorism. Even small rumours of nuclear threats and folk begin survival stockpiling. Some even enter suicide pacts in preparation for the end times. Conspiracy theories in social media or the newspapers provoke, in fact *control*, public panic.

These epic scenarios on a large canvas have the power to feed an over-anxious psyche with apocalyptic dread. The word 'apocalypse' means an event of destruction on an awesome or catastrophic scale. The apocalypse describes what is to come and signals the end of all things and the world as we know it. History is brought to a cataclysmic end by the winding up of this present age in terrifying scenes.

Hollywood is a past master at titillating our appetite for chilling apocalyptic films: *Armageddon* (1998), *The Day after Tomorrow* (2004),

Children of Men (2006), *I am Legend* (2007), *2012* (2009), *The Maze Runner* (2014), *These Final Hours* (2014), *Mad Max: Fury Road* (2015), *Apocalypse* (2017) — to name but a few. George R. R. Martin's series of epic fantasy novels, *A Song of Ice and Fire* starts with the first book, *Game of Thrones*, and the beginning of a blockbuster fantasy drama television series. Practically everyone has a dark and unsettling prophecy: a young beautiful queen will ascend to power, three children will die, and so on. These prophecies drive and shape the story and its characters.

Science sometimes teases our readiness for uneasiness or disquiet. Will there be vaccines to withstand a national (probably global) flu epidemic? Will climate change precipitate the premature end of the earth *in our day*? The press had a field day with the European Centre for Nuclear Research (CERN) and the Hadron Collider experiments — the worry about creating black holes, and the disastrous consequences for the universe.

In the arts, soothsayers abound. Lines from the rock classic *The Sound of Silence* (allegedly written by Simon and Garfunkel in a bathroom with the lights turned off), tell us that 'the people bowed and prayed to the neon God they made', and that 'the words of the prophets are written on the subway walls and tenement halls.'

The American poet Allen Ginsberg ranted and raved as a voice for the Beat Generation of the Sixties. His poem 'Howl' (scrawled in cafés) was a deliberate outrage: explicit homosexuality, pornography, drugs, a money-grabbing industrial machine, a nation laid waste and 'the best minds of our generation' destroyed. The great American Dream pulverised by a gigantic shrug—Whatever! 'Howl' overcame censorship to become one of the most widely read poems of the twentieth century.

The universities roll the dice too. Three days after the US presidential election in 2016, a sharp law professor tweeted words from a book published nearly two decades previously. Thousands of retweets sent the book's Amazon ranking skyrocketing, spawning a run on it, so that by the end of that day, *Achieving Our Country* was no longer available and had been rushed for reprinting. Why the stampede?

Richard Rorty, an American pragmatist philosopher died nearly a decade before the shock election of Donald Trump. Yet he accurately foretold the rise of a 'strongman' to fight the corner of the nonsuburban electorate (unskilled and badly educated, unhappy with exported jobs), who decide that the system (smug bureaucrats, tricky lawyers and white-collar college graduates) had failed them.

From these few examples, we see that our world likes to comment or voice an opinion on life and that sometimes (scrubbing out the ridiculous) this could be 'prophetic', but only in a worldly sense. It is not strictly Christian prophecy, which is Christ speaking and, therefore, in Christian prophecy we must know beyond a shadow of a doubt that the source of the voice is Christ.

Secondly, we see what's trending in the adventurous seekers of oracles who believe that there is something 'out there', desirous of communicating with us. And some being from the 'other side' does invariably show itself through a medium of some sort. It may well be a spiritualist in a trance in a séance, or table tapping, or automatic writing (words written by another hand), or spiritual voices and spectral, ghostly illusions from the dead. Some learn Eastern methods of channelling spiritual gurus from the past, or of connecting to the power of Ascended Masters with special energies. Some people live according to the symbols they find in numbers, codes, the stars, palmistry, or tarot cards. Others find messages in crystals, trees or stones. Quite a few actually *see* physical apparitions or angels and hear voices in dreams.

Many are cynical of such spiritual forces and question their validity. Are the so-called mediums merely charlatans out for financial gain from the naïve? Are these techniques simply powers of suggestion, or autosuggestion, or mass hypnosis? Are there otherworldly powers at work? Is there something dark behind it all?

I live a few miles from Avebury, the world's largest pre-historic stone circle and a World Heritage Site. The colossal standing stones have immense drawing power, especially at the

Summer and Winter Solstices where there can be up to 30,000 visitors. Many camp as close to the stones as possible, hugging the stones and dancing through the stones to welcome the sun. They believe that there are mystic vibrations in the air, in the atmosphere, in the very ground itself. And on a balmy summer's night in the chalk grassland, low-flung stars touching earth, or in the frosty cold of a pre-dawn dark it seems credible. Devotees are convinced and who is to say they are wrong? However, even if enough believe that the stones still speak or that UFOs are sighted or that crop circles have materialised spontaneously, then does their authority make these things credible?

EXAMINING THE SOURCE

For analysts of our world, or for New Age teachings, just about anything goes, providing it sounds credible or feels good. We care little for fixed convention. That's totally boring. Old thoughts and ways of belief — utterly boring. Our post-truth generation *loves* pick-and-mix. Exciting ideas are swapped and exchanged as readily as night follows day. So that when it comes to the world religions, we could argue that all say more or less the same thing, as they are all going the same way anyway! All are awash with prophesying, messianic beliefs, paradise, cycles of time, destruction and rebuilding of the earth, a new heaven. All these ideas are found in Islam,

Zoroastrianism, Buddhism, Jainism, Baha'ism, Judeo-Christianity and Hinduism.

However, according to the writer of the Letter to the Hebrews we are *not* all on the same path and hearing the same voice because, for Christians, Jesus Christ is the supreme revelation:

> Long ago God spoke to our ancestors in many and various ways by the prophets, but in these last days he has spoken to us by a Son ... He is the reflection of God's glory and the exact imprint of God's very being, and he sustains all things by his powerful word.

Hebrews 1:1–3

The Christian belief is that God has spoken uniquely and once for all through his Son. Jesus Christ upstages all voices. He is centre stage as *the* final Word from God who sustains everything he created.

Let us see how the uniqueness of Jesus' voice plays out in the dramatic story of a young Indian, a Hindu Sikh called Sundar Singh (1889–1933). His mother brought him up to believe that God speaks in many ways and in every faith. Her early death is a shock for Sundar. He rebels against his Christian school and publically burns the Bible in a fit of rage.

On a certain day, in utter turmoil and in the depths of despair he takes a vow that, unless

God speaks to him before five a.m. he will hurl himself under the Rampur express train. This is a nail-biting contest! The minutes tick by. Suddenly, at a quarter to five, Sundar hurtles out of his room and declares for all to hear that the face and figure of Jesus had come in a bright cloud of light, right into his room. Jesus had spoken to him in Hindustani and he, Sundar, had fallen at His feet!

What drama, what a conversion to the living Jesus. Sundar rejects his Hindu past and refuses to mix the two religions. He will not submit to Hindu traditions despite relentless pressure from his family, even to the point of their trying to poison him. He survives! However, his refusal to renounce Christianity condemns Sundar Singh to a life of exile. He is formally cut off from his natural family and, stripped of all human belonging, he dons the yellow robe of a Hindu sadhu (a holy man) and becomes a missionary to India.

Sundar's total allegiance and utter submission to Christ is the catapult for the preaching of the gospel as the prophet travels to Tibet, North and South India, the Buddhist states, the British colony of Ceylon, Australia, America and Great Britain (a leper colony is part of the journey).

The testimony of Sundar Singh is that Jesus spoke to him and that his voice was the authoritative divine word. Ha! A sceptic might argue: merely the figment of a fertile imagination. Take the young lad to a psychiatrist and help him get over his mother's death and his desire to escape reality. Clearly, the voice of Jesus is the projection of an overactive imagination or thyroid designed to 'get me out of here' as fast as possible.

A sceptic disbelieves accepted opinions and throws doubt on the Christian story, fighting tooth and nail against its credibility. A sceptical position takes its stand against all the accumulated intelligence in the best of all Christian encounter and endeavour throughout the last two millennia. A sceptic considers that the material world, that which can be observed touched and examined, is the only reality. The rest is the stuff of dreams. Unscientific. Prehistoric. Primitive. Dark Ages. Myth. Superstition. Untrustworthy.

A relativist (a person who thinks that truth is not absolute and that there are many truths) will say that was okay for Sundar Singh, but someone else may see an angel, or an apparition, or a ghostbuster. Who is to say that Jesus' voice is the only one? And they would be right: there are many voices, as we have seen. But that the word of Jesus is the *final* authority ... now *that* is the sticking point. Certainly, for Sundar Singh it was. And it still is for the many millions who have come to know Jesus Christ as Lord of all. But for countless others, his voice is one among many.

EXAMINING THE HEART

Outside the retreat villa in the brilliant sunshine of an Umbrian spring, a visiting elderly cultured Italian (a lapsed Catholic) holds my attention: our world needs God and all peoples of all faiths should return to God's ways. He is quick to point out that it really doesn't matter which God, and best not to mention the name of Jesus Christ. For the sake of a peaceful universe we should avoid all conflict between religions.

These are common beliefs held today by many. What, then, shall Christians do? Shall we abandon religion (after all, it only leads to wars), and especially the testimony of Jesus Christ (reactionary, conservative, peculiar, old-fashioned, a bore), in the hope that by some other means the world shall be put to rights? It may even be a question of adapt or die. Adapt to the tepid spiritual climate or die to the truth of Christ.

Christians might adapt to the relativist and settle for a mixed economy. Embrace the many voices and deny the particularity of Jesus Christ. A little bit of this, a little bit of that. Or Christians might surrender to the total onslaught on belief and give in to the sceptic, to the voice of doubt. And so dies the truth once believed. That Christians should neither adapt nor die, but hold fast the belief that Jesus Christ *is* the way, the truth, and the life, is an extremely unpopular notion.

When Christians stand their ground to contend for the faith handed down, they invariably draw the short straw in a religious discussion or debate. At this point, when short of answers, how invaluable is fresh revelation of the matter at hand! This is where prophecy comes into its own. Christians share in the interpretation of God's heart and will, and learn how to unveil what has been hidden.

For this reason, the Bible puts an extremely high value on prophecy. In the Old Testament, we find Moses wishing that 'all were prophets' (Num 11:30), and in the New Testament we read that prophecy is the gift to be desired above all others: 'Pursue love and strive for the spiritual gifts, and especially that you may prophesy' (1 Cor 14:1).

We know that Paul means what he says, since he uses a particular Greek construct in this verse and in verse 5 ('Now I would like all of you to speak in tongues, but even more to prophesy'). The phrases 'especially that' and 'even more' translate the Greek construct *mallon de*, which signifies a constant increase: 'much more' or 'still more, and more and more'. The force of argument is carried by repetition. Paul is shouting out: Seek all the spiritual gifts, but more strongly, long to prophesy!

The logic behind Paul's adamance is that 'those

who prophesy speak to other people for their upbuilding and encouragement and consolation ... those who prophesy build up the church (vv.3-4).' It is quite clear that prophecy is incredibly useful to the church as it strengthens and directs God's purposes. And all this revelation comes by means of ordinary people, who by nature are simply incapable of thinking or imagining God's thoughts.

QUESTIONS FOR FURTHER DISCUSSION

Are you drawn to see the future by means of any of the ways mentioned? Is this still something you readily practise?

Have you ever experienced a prophetic intervention, an insight given by the Spirit of God, so that you knew how to respond to a difficult question?

Does your church encourage the gift of prophecy? If not, how could prophecy be encouraged?

2

SPOTTING THE SIGNPOSTS: TEST FIRST

In the previous chapter, we examined ways in which our world worries about future shock and is taken up with many voices. Christians want to hear God's voice, but this is proving to be even more difficult than before since the onset of the digital revolution.

We multitask: the mobile phone on loudspeaker, a frying pan in one hand, one eye on the laptop on the kitchen table, music on digital radio or in the ether on WiFi, and snippets of news from the television in the other room. A teen on a skateboard, headphones in ears, messaging a friend; a commuter on a bus or train, newspaper tucked into a case, Kindle to hand, mobile bleeping text and e-mail, stock prices and the weather, syncing watch and phone; iPad and iPod blend eyes and ears in a seamless togetherness. We are trapped on a highway of congested sound.

Like the noise of dozens of traders on the manic floor of a stock exchange, many voices shout out in a clamour for our attention. Noise. And, more specifically, white noise – many frequencies with equal intensities – is our barrier to the voice of God.

> I saw a robed clergyman at the noonday service of Holy Communion in a famous English Cathedral, hard-pressed to make himself heard over the voice of a tour guide—and this despite a very loud microphone.

If, however, we do manage to hear a messenger over this cacophony of sound, our next problem is whether it is true. How do we test the message? Of course, the first test of genuine prophecy is that it comes true. It must be accurate. Prophecy, knowing the mind of the Lord, goes ahead to speak of what is to come:

> You may say to yourself, 'How can we recognize a word that the Lord has not spoken?' If a prophet speaks in the name of the Lord but the thing does not take place or prove true, it is a word that the Lord has not spoken. The prophet has spoken it presumptuously; do not be frightened by it.
> **Deuteronomy 18:21–22**

I suggest that we can learn to spot three signposts to the genuine Christian prophecy: i) that it conforms to the Bible; ii) it testifies to Jesus Christ and the Holy Spirit; and iii) it is open to dreams and visions. And, lest we jump up and down about the last pointer: in that very same famous English cathedral, I was in the congregation squashed into the choir stalls on the Feast of the Epiphany and heard the preacher tell us all about a vision of an angel and how we should be open to these visitations as they are perfectly scriptural.

ONE SACRED TEXT

Our first test then must be the Holy Bible, the only sacred text for Christians. All true prophecy agrees with the revelation in Scripture and can be checked against the witness of Scripture, its commands, its prohibitions, and its warnings.

In Cape Town, South Africa, I once heard a prophetess from a mainstream church speaking on her grand tour of many churches. She was endorsed by the highest authority in her denomination. Seated in an overflow room and watching her via video link, I became increasingly uncomfortable. As far as I could fathom, her words seemed not to ring true to the biblical witness in two aspects.

The first, her prophecies were received through automatic writing. In other words, her pen was controlled, not by herself but by another, as she wrote down the messages. This is not the case with the Old Testament prophets. Certainly, the text states that the hand of the Lord was upon them in power, but there is no evidence that God physically controlled their writing. The prophets or their scribes themselves wrote out the words they received.

The second, her prophecies managed to insert the Virgin Mary into the Godhead so that the Trinity was comprised not of three but of four persons. This view is unscriptural and not consistent with the teaching of the Church. Thankfully, a few years later I read that the prophetess had been exposed by her denomination as a fraud.

The parable of the sheepfold tells us that the sheep listen to the voice of the good shepherd but run away from the voices of sheep stealers — the frauds, tricksters and impersonators of God (John 10:1-16). We are also told that Satan masquerades as an angel of light and, thus disguised, attempts to lead the saints into false idolatry (2 Cor 11:14).

An example of this deception is the current cultural fascination with angels, perhaps best played out in Robbie Williams' fantastic hit song, 'Angels'. In it, angels are both human and divine, reside up above and down below, can be spirit guides, departed loved ones or guardians for our problems. Does this fit the biblical story? Unfortunately, our rather worldly picture of angels is not only naïve, but unchristian.

The Bible tells us that angels cannot be personal guides or friends to those on earth. Angels cannot be called up, summoned at will or spoken to as though they were human. In fact, if perchance we bumped into one we would probably be terrified out of our wits!

In the following passage, the prophet is reprimanded for falling down to worship the angel:

> Then I fell down at his feet to worship him, but he said to me, "You must not do that! I am a fellow servant with you and your comrades who hold the testimony of Jesus. Worship God!
> **Revelation 19:10**

It is strictly forbidden to idolise or worship angels. Angels worship God and point us to Christ. At his nativity, we see their brilliance as the heavenly host glorifies and honours the babe, the uncreated and pre-existent Son of God come to earth as Saviour. Angels were created by God for the express purpose of being his heavenly messengers and throughout Scripture we see that they operate only at his command. Believing that my 'personal angel' has conversations with me and guides me daily is biblically unfounded, cannot be prophecy, and is to be avoided by Christians.

Yet we do long for guidance. When I was a teenager I found a book on palmistry and my curiosity led me to trace my life line, my time of death and my leadership abilities on my hands. Fascinating! I began to believe in, and to be controlled by what I saw. I played with my horoscope, allowing my star to dictate my character. When I learned to give in to Jesus Christ as the Lord of my life I got rid of this stuff and trusted God for the way he had created me and for my life choices. However compelling they might be, all divination – numerology or palmistry, fortune telling, sorcery and astrology – are examples of false guidance. The Devil can, and does, mimic God.

The New Testament warns us about listening to spiritual entities which enslave a person before conversion to Christ:

> Formerly, when you did not know God, you were enslaved to beings that by nature are not gods. Now, however, that you have come to know God, or rather to be known by God, how can you turn back again to the weak and beggarly elemental spirits? How can you want to be enslaved to them again?
> **Galatians 4:8–11**

The words, 'weak and beggarly elemental spirits' translate a Greek word, *stoicheia*. The word *stoicheia* occurs often in literature and, in the following texts is translated in different ways but always as forces opposed to God. *Stoicheia* are 'elemental (Gal 4:8–11), 'so-called' gods (1 Cor 8:5), 'no-gods' or 'dumb idols' (1 Cor 12:2). *Stoicheia* exercise a sinister, even demonic influence (1 Cor 8:7). The word *stoicheia* refers also to the power of human words, those which trap by 'philosophy and empty deceit, according to human tradition, according to the elemental spirits [*stoicheia*] of the universe, and not according to Christ' (Col 2:8–9). This means that words, regardless of their source, exercise power and sometimes can be evil. We have only to think of the rousing speeches of Adolf Hitler to understand this concept. His words galvanised an entire nation to believe a lie.

How do these 'other gods' impact on prophecy? Greatly. These biblical passages warn us that they are pagan entities which speak deceptively. These spirits are not from God and they speak with a false voice (see Jer 14:14, 23:16). They seduce away from allegiance to Jesus Christ. They can lead to paganism, to the worship of the natural elements of earth, wind, fire and water.

We find these elements in the true story of Axel Munthe (*The Story of San Michele*), a fashionable Parisian doctor who, charmed by the intoxicating beauty of the Italian island of Capri, sets out to restore a Roman villa to its former glory. In the garden, he is beguiled by a phantom from the past, a tall figure wrapped in a rich mantle, wreathed in an ancient wraithlike spirit world. In exchange for all the glory and grandeur he craves, Munthe must surrender his soul to the dark god of this island. And he does. The villa's restoration makes a stir and the sleepy island becomes a honey pot for the rich and famous, who bring with them toys of seduction: drugs, pornography, sexual freedoms.

At this juncture, you may object: surely you are not saying that everything that is not Jesus is evil? Clearly this cannot be so. Of course, anyone may bring a message and it could be inspired by

God or it may be their own thought. This is not evil. It is their own thinking. However, when we are testing voices from a 'supernatural, not of this world' realm, we ought to be clear about their source. Either they are from God and his angelic kingdom or they are of Satan and his demonic kingdom. There can be nothing in between. A pure and holy God and his pure and holy kingdom simply cannot include any work of darkness or impurity.

TWO HANDS OF GOD

The second test is to ask how God himself is involved in prophecy and the act of prophesying. To help us imagine how God might work, we use an image first coined by a theologian of the early Church, Irenaeus (c.200). He uses the phrase, 'the two hands of God' to refer to Jesus Christ and the Holy Spirit who work *together* as agents on God's mission. The Word and the Spirit are both there at the creation of the world, and they are both there at its recreation in the cross and resurrection. The two hands do the will of the Father. We see this synergy, this working together in the gift of prophecy. How?

Prophecy shows the hand of Jesus working in the following way. It stands to reason that, just as a small child recognises a parent in a message given to the school secretary ('Sorry darling, going to be late as Nanna Anna's not well'), so a prophetic message ought to be the sort of thing

God would say. It should sound like God. It should be like him and show his character.

This brings us to Jesus Christ whom, we have seen, is God's exact representation and image. Jesus said, 'Whoever has seen me has seen the Father' (John 14:9). The character of Jesus should be in the prophecy shining forth the very nature of God. When this is the case we see the hand of the Word of God at work.

The revelation of Jesus is not, however, automatic. A second factor is required, God's other hand, his secret agent the Spirit of prophecy. For just as the Holy Spirit inspired Scripture, a great deal of which is prophetic writing, so he inspires the ongoing witness to Jesus Christ:

> No prophecy of scripture is a matter of one's own interpretation, because no prophecy ever came by human will, but men and women moved by the Holy Spirit spoke from God.
> **2 Peter 1:20–21**

When a prophecy testifies to Jesus, then it is the prophetic Spirit speaking. The two hands of God work together; or, put another way, 'the testimony of Jesus is the Spirit of prophecy' (Rev 19:10).

How does this work in practice? A prophetic message must testify to Jesus and sound like something Jesus might have said or done. This makes it a revelation because it is revealing something about Jesus, his character, his words of life. This revelation should be bursting with the energy and impulse of the Spirit of God. The Spirit is empowering the Word of Christ. The two hands are working together.

For example, a lady gets up in a church meeting and tells everyone that they are greatly loved by the Lord (which we have heard many times, it must be said), but then she continues to speak and now there is something different. Under the prompt of the Holy Spirit, she expands the word and begins to speak directly to those present whose hearts may have become lukewarm.

She says that the Lord desires to set a fire, in fact a furnace in these hearts. Now we listen up, could it be me? And then, as the woman prophesying is moved by the Holy Spirit, she receives a picture: a lukewarm heart is enfolded in the warm hands of Jesus. This picture, together with the word, inspire those who can say: She's talking about me! They respond – perhaps going forward for prayer or praying in their seats – asking God to rekindle a first love. The word of Christ, plus the movement of the Spirit work *together* to invigorate believers. Spot on!

The messenger of this hypothetical prophecy is a Christian, in Christ and led by the Spirit. There is no evidence in the Bible that prophecy is given by an unbeliever. We may experience God speaking to us through many different means: a line in a song, a piece of music, a poem, a donkey (see Num 22:21–31)! Even a wily Jewish politician like Caiaphas can speak, not on his own authority, 'but being high priest that year he prophesied that Jesus was about to die for the nation, and not for the nation only, but to gather into one the dispersed children of God' (John 11:51–52).

God uses that person or circumstance unbeknownst to them. However, when a well-meaning messenger sprouts forth homegrown words, they might sound good, even inspired, but do not pass the test of Word and Spirit and, therefore, cannot be classified as prophecy.

The test of Word and Spirit can also be applied to dreams and visions. Do they point to Jesus? Are they created by the Holy Spirit? Mostly our dreams are not prophetic or of God. Mainly they originate in the subconscious as we detox the day or replay the past. Some are sent by powers of darkness to frighten and disturb us. And sometimes we dream in God. These prophetic dreams leave us with hope, or a warning, or guidance, or simply a feeling of peace and well-being. We wake knowing that the Lord has spoken to us and are assured of his loving presence.

Scripture is packed with dreams and dreamers. People changed nations by dreams. Remember Joseph in Egypt and Pharaoh's cows? Or Daniel in Babylon and Nebuchadnezzar's great statue? People were instructed by dreams. Joseph and Mary's pregnancy, Joseph and the flight to

Egypt. We should not be wary of prophetic dreams but welcome them by faith.

Visions are harder to pin down. They, too, can be figments of imagination and untrustworthy. We are commanded not to dwell on the vision which puffs up with pride (Col 2:18). We are to stick to Scripture and not be tempted to live life via vision. Prophets who speak lies and rely on dreams and visions are rebuked outright (see Jer 23). But when God does speak in a vision and all heaven breaks loose in my heart, I am fired up and blessed.

> In the middle of a lengthy sermon, a friend had a vision: Jesus was in her home and garden as it became a place of refuge and peace. Being recently moved and on the lookout for a new church of belonging, this vision came as a great blessing as it shifted her perspective inwards and away from the somewhat urgent tyranny of the business of finding a church.

We shall look at three visions of three tree trunks as signposts to discerning Christian prophecy.

THREE TREE TRUNKS

Most of us are familiar with the video camera (from the Latin verb *video*, 'I see'). The word 'vision' (from the Latin noun, *visio*) is part of this group of Latin words to do with seeing or sight. Think about a video on your camera or mobile phone, or even a dated video recorder. Recently, I watched a short black and white holiday video, recorded by my father of his three small children running and shouting in the grounds of a Zimbabwean hotel. It was so funny to watch and it brought back such memories. In the same way, a vision can be moving or stationary, in technicolour or black and white. It can last nanoseconds or hours. It can be external, seen outside one's brain or body, or internal and seen in one's spirit.

One still, mild April noonday in 2012, in the garden of a retreat house – a villa nestled among Umbrian hills – I was praying. I had a fervent hope that God would speak to me in this 'thin place.' The ancient Celts used the phrase, 'thin places' to describe spellbinding sites (windswept Iona, the aloof island of Skellig Michael) where the distance between heaven and earth feels shorter and they seem to give way to one another so that the divine seems transparently real.

As I meditated, I saw quite clearly in my mind's eye, and in colour, a sequence of three tree trunks. The first was very, very old. Colossal. Its immense girth sustained by a system of thickset, gnarled roots plunged deeply into the earth. The second tree trunk, at first glance, appeared to be out of shape. Looking more intently, I saw that it was throne-shaped like a sort of half moon and that a person sat comfortably within it, but attached and part of the tree itself. The third was a tree stump whose roots were invisible, but it was brimming with life and sprouting little green shoots.

What could be the meaning of this vision of three tree trunks, which had come so unexpectedly out of the blue—left field? Going indoors, I prayed and found myself recalling scriptures, and then the three parts of the vision fell into place. As I meditated, I understood that each tree trunk represents a spiritual state and a way of attaining divine knowledge or wisdom.

The first tree trunk goes all the way back to the Garden of Eden (that ancient root system I had seen) and the warning to the first pair not to eat of the tree of the knowledge of good and evil (Gen 1-3): If you eat this fruit you will be separated from God and you will die. Adam and Eve disobeyed and were expelled from Paradise, satiated with the knowledge of both good and evil.

Christianity teaches that this story represents all our stories and that we are all 'fallen' from innocence. Their far-from-God state is ours too. We are all alienated from God and in need of rescue. Once we have received Jesus' gift of salvation we find our way back to God. Nevertheless, despite our freedom as newly born children of God, we are still free – in that open state of freewill – to feed on any kind of knowledge. And we do, both good and bad.

What, then, does human freedom have to do with the gift of prophecy? Much in every way. Because of the knowledge of good and evil which we now possess, we are free to prophesy stuff which can be, and sometimes is, a mixture of God and self. We do not always see and hear God clearly; our view of divine things is flawed. We prophesy in part, with only a partial knowledge of God and, therefore, our prophecy can be inaccurate, tainted as it is by the fallen self. Think of a drainpipe pouring out clean water mixed with impurities: our speech can be clogged with impure thoughts and words, even when we are disciples of Jesus Christ.

I'm working in a café at the foot of the stupendous fourteenth century ruin of Carreg Cennen Castle in west Wales when I catch a snippet of conversation at the next table. It seems to have some bearing on the paragraph I've just written on the knowledge of good and evil. Two friends are discussing a contemporary author and the blurring of the good and bad in the characters described, making it hard to distinguish who's who in the novels. Who are the good and who are the bad? In the same way, prophecy can be a mix of good and bad stuff.

The second vision, a tree trunk shaped like a throne, showed the seated person as part of the tree itself. Here is an I-throne, an enthroned self. Paul depicts his tussle, to which we can relate, rather poignantly: 'For I do not do the good I want, but the evil I do not want is what I do'

(Rom 7:15). Here is the power of self chained to itself, to its own desires. This is a state of self-dependency. An I-throne roots all knowledge in the self and these roots go deeply into the soil of generations of independence from God. Here I am seated on my throne, master of my destiny and captain of my soul. Such knowledge is power.

The exalted ego, high and lifted up, worshipped and adored, is marvellously portrayed in Shakespeare's Cleopatra. The unrivalled celebrity queen for Mark Antony's love is enthroned in Egyptian gorgeousness and fêted by the very air she breathes:

> The barge she sat in,
> like a burnished throne,
> Burnt on the water.
> The poop was beaten gold;
> Purple the sails, and so perfumèd that
> The winds were love-sick with them …
> **Antony and Cleopatra, 2.2.198–201**

Here is beguiling beauty, bewitching sexual prowess, breathtaking power. The entire city has gone after her. To such idols, we bow to worship; to these thrones, we bend the knee, raising kissing lips of adoration to gods and goddesses. You are a god, I am a god, we are gods, we are the champions!

When it comes to prophesying, the warning of the I-throne is plain. Prophecy centred in the self is wrong. Prophesying, however grand it appears, which exalts the self and not God, must be idolatry. Celebrity prophets are out! In our socially networked world this is a hard lesson. And after all Jesus was something of a celeb. The whole world went after him. And that was okay, because he is God himself and so shines with all that is in and of God. But we are *not* God; we must point *to* God. And that is the secret of prophesying.

The problem of idolatry and prophesying is very much with us today. When prophetic vision goes pear-shaped we may find at its core the power of the idol. May we learn from observing a beehive: a virgin queen bee favoured above all workers and drones and able to sting all rival queens without dying. There was that mega church with a prophetic leader queen bee, protected by aide-de-camps from every rival vision, until the cracks in the fabric gave way to her divorce and the collapse of a family empire.

Thankfully, in contrast with these two unreliable tree trunks, the third vision brings us to the purity of the spiritual wisdom which is in Christ Jesus. The budding tree stump with hidden roots is a direct reference to a messianic prophecy in Isaiah 11:1:

> A shoot shall come out from the stump of Jesse,
> and a branch shall grow out of his roots.
> **Isaiah 11:1**

The meaning of this passage is straightforward. The stump or trunk refers to the ancestral lineage of Jesse, the father of David, who ruled as king gloriously over Israel. The branch which grows out of these roots is the Messiah, whom Christians call Jesus Christ, born of the house of David. The attributes of Messiah, on whom the Spirit of the Lord rests, are set out as wisdom, understanding, counsel, might, knowledge, and awesome fear of God (Isa 11:2). From Messiah comes all that is true and necessary to know God. And this none more so when it comes to divinely inspired prophesying, whose source is the wisdom of Christ.

In the hilly town of Anacapri, up, up the winding road from the villa of Axel Munthe, we have a high-spirited discussion about Christ and philosophy over a glass of wine and home-produced Insalata Capresa. My friends are born and bred on Capri and love philosophic speculation.

We compare English and Italian translations, where the New Testament declares emphatically that Jesus is superlative and far above the Greek and Jewish debaters and scribes of his day: 'Christ the power of God and the wisdom of God' (1 Cor 1:24). We decide that this statement has universal application and holds true for every age. Truly, Christ Jesus 'became for us wisdom from God' (1 Cor. 1:30).

However, this point, that Jesus has *uniquely* revealed God, is hotly contested, especially when it comes to words of wisdom from the sages and holy men down the ages. On my early morning run through the heights of Capri I pass through Parco Filosofico (the park of the philosophers), dedicated to Roman and Greek wisdom, to thinkers from Confucius to Nietzsche and on to the rather precarious cliff edge. Inscribed on a rock is a random thought by the philosopher Immanuel Kant: 'Two things inspire me to awe – the starry heavens above and the moral universe within.' My eyes turn from an azure sky above and then drop down, down, hundreds of feet of sheer rock to a shimmering sea below. Later I discover that this lookout point, devoted to philosophy, is infamous for suicides.

The vision of the three trees makes us think about sources of wisdom. Naturally, we do not discount insights from thinkers down the ages, but Jesus Christ is *more than* them. He is not a mere guru like Buddha or Krishna (those wise men from the East came seeking *him*, after all), or simply a wise teacher like Socrates. His radiation is greater than Pharaoh's sun. He is not a spark of the Divine in the way of the New Age. He does not offer philosophical discourse in the method of Descartes or Kant, nor the rationality of a great leader or statesman, nor the intellectual achievements of poets, scientists, artists, entrepreneurs or philanthropists.

Obviously, in the affairs of the world, we are ruled by all kinds of good sense, brilliant reasoning and collective learning. None of these may be remotely connected to God, although they may speak of God's character indirectly. For Christians seeking to prophesy, these snippets of godly truth in our human striving should not content us. We are after revelation—the idea that the Lord reveals and discloses his mind *without our aid*.

This chapter has endeavoured to find a way through the maze of discerning prophecies: the deviations and distractions, the devils and deceit, the self-motivated and self-centred. Ultimately it is Christ who is wisdom, the speaker of divine truth. His word is unmixed and pure. Prophecies which speak in the purity of Christ – testify to his character, are touched by the power of the Holy Spirit and avoid the pitfalls of puffed up conceit – are the real McCoy, trustworthy and true.

QUESTIONS FOR FURTHER DISCUSSION

Have you (or someone you know) ever heard voices from a 'supernatural not of this world realm'? What did they sound like? Were they true or false?

Have you listened to a prophetic message where it was plain that both hands of God – Jesus Christ and the Holy Spirit – were present? How did you know this?

Are you comfortable with the idea of vision? Have you had a vision?

3

STRENGTHENING THE CHURCH: PROPHECY FIRST

In this mad sea of faith and unfaith, we may well ask why the Church does not leap more often into the maelstrom of mixed messages, bringing strengthening prophecy. Sometimes the Church seems rather quiet, not talking about God's stuff in a very loud voice, but only in a small voice or not at all. And yet when God's voice does penetrate our dullness, it is so very helpful.

At a Friday vigil before Pentecost Sunday, in a twelfth century abbey, there was a prophetic word from the Lord: 'I am in control.' On Saturday night, people on London Bridge and Borough Market in central London were the targets of a knife and van terror attack. Very recently, I heard of a vicar's wife who, being fired by a prophetic word from a friend for their area, leaped out of bed on a Saturday morning, hared down to the venue of a women's conference in their town and delivered the message. It was well received and, no doubt, became a topic of prayer for the area.

It may be a surprise to learn that there are huge swathes of the Church who take the gift of prophecy very seriously indeed. On 22nd April

2017 a prophetic call from a respected South African farmer went out: 'It's Time!' And on that day, a million Christians flocked together to a farm (by foot, buses, taxis, cars, camper vans, and four hundred aeroplanes). They came from all over the country to pray: 'We are tired of people taking the law into their own hands. We are going to call upon the Lord to bring justice, peace and hope to our beloved South Africa' (Angus Buchan).

In this chapter, we will look at a Church stream which is utterly sold out on prophecy first, before turning to the reliable mainstream (traditional denominations), and then to the energetic evangelical-charismatic-pentecostal stream.

SOLD OUT ON PROPHECY FIRST

The practices of the Pentecostal church may not be our style, but the fact remains that Pentecostalism was the fastest growing religion of the twentieth century and has steadily taken ground throughout the world. In Europe, it has been resisted (apart from small Protestant congregations), but everywhere else it has flourished.

Pentecostalism is marked by its small-group meetings, the empowerment of people with the gifts of the Holy Spirit, liberation for women and justice issues. To Pentecostal churches, the business of putting prophecy first comes perfectly naturally. To the outsider, it looks chaotic: loud noisy praying, even shouting, tongue-speaking all together and crying out, bold unrestrained prophesying out loud.

Perhaps this stuff is only for the emotionally unstable or insecure? Pentecostals would object strongly to that dismissive take on their church. For them, the prophetic experience is *essential* in training disciples of Jesus. *Knowing* the Lord means *growing* in Him. The gifts of the Spirit are not optional extras but foundational for the Christian's growth. Miracles, healings and prophecies are part and parcel of a dynamic experience of God in the power of the Holy Spirit.

Pentecostals believe that the Spirit speaks just as easily to ordinary people as to leaders. *Anyone* can hear the Lord directly and clearly *for themselves*. During worship, there is an expectation that the Spirit will touch the heart and there is no fear of deep-seated emotion as the Lord brings something of himself to them. This might be through a picture or mental image, or a prophetic 'word'. Sometimes there is a 'nudge', a perceptive sense of how the Spirit is working in a meeting. This 'report' reveals the heart of those present: an affliction or distress of some sort, or guidance for the perplexed.

Congregations are hardwired to these 'nudges' from the Holy Spirit, perceiving them as prophetic promptings. An individual, or the whole group, receives a revelation, often when the very voice of God seems to sound forth in inspired prophetic preaching, the impact of which can be felt tangibly — even in the sober Church of England!

A participant in the Pentecost Sunday morning congregation at the above-mentioned abbey, electrified by the powerful sermon on Acts 2, involuntarily began to pray in tongues and, quite overcome, had to leave the dignified proceedings and head for the car park to continue praying in the car.

Pentecostals rate this unusual gift of 'speaking in tongues' or 'praying in tongues', found in passages in the Book of Acts and 1 Corinthians. This is an inspired prayer language, given by God, where words or sounds unknown to the person are uttered out loud. Usually, this sort of prayer is for private intimate communion with God, but there can be a wave of corporate tongue speaking or singing together in tongues in gatherings. Sometimes, in a public setting someone speaks in tongues and then there is an interpretation. It turns out to be a message for a single person or for the meeting. This, too, is prophecy. Pentecostals view the gift of tongues as the beginning of prophecy, as it opens the human spirit to the workings of the Holy Spirit.

Two friends were enjoying a cup of tea in an upmarket café, when a woman seated on a sofa opposite proceeded to have a fit. Undaunted, one of them began to pray quietly but out loud in tongues. The woman calmed down after a while, told them that she had a lapsed Christian faith and that she had heard her name called by the one praying in tongues. The friends knew that the Lord had spoken to her in the tongue and they were able to encourage her faith!

Interestingly, reliable sources tell us that the nuns in the twelfth century Benedictine community in Rupertsberg speak to one another in a spiritual language. As their abbess is the powerful prophetess and mystic, Hildegard of Bingen, this may come as no great surprise.

The Pentecostal way of listening to the Spirit goes from the gathered assembly to the private devotions, and to when two or three pray together. Here is that mysterious encounter, that 'meeting with the Lord' where a life-changing connection to Jesus is made. And this personal transformation is the fountainhead to affect the community.

Essentially, Pentecostal people are missionaries modelled on the early Church in the Book of Acts. The Holy Spirit spearheads the mission, empowering people for works of witness in very obvious ways. Gifts of wisdom and revelation in vision and dream are for the salvation of others. But they are also for the restoration of the whole person or an entire community. The Pentecostal Church *is* a prophetic community in the world. It wants to be involved in works of service or justice in an holistic manner and prophecies can help to point up areas of need in neighbourhoods and nations

Unfortunately, it is not always the case that Pentecostal churches stick to their guns about the gifts of the Spirit. Today, there are some who have tired of the supernatural interventions by the Spirit and whose churches are simply copycats of good business practice. There are also practices within the stream which cause many in the mainstream, to which we now turn, to be highly suspicious: the flogging of a prosperity gospel (turn to Jesus and get rich, become a millionaire, God wants to increase your wealth); the forcible financial fleecing of supporters (minsters get richer and richer; irresponsible use of peoples' tithes and offerings); power dynamics (leaders on show, exhibitionism and control of congregations).

Abuse of power and overemphasis of one or the other doctrine can often give Pentecostalism a bad reputation. This is a great pity. The Pentecostal stream gives the worldwide Church a vibrant legacy of New Testament mission.

NOT SOLD OUT ON PROPHECY

That's all well and good for *those* sorts of churches but we are the traditional middle-of-the-road mainstream. We have to remain sane and relevant to our society without any shenanigans and goings-on. We are believers in the Trinity: Father, Son and Holy Spirit.

Of course, we believe in the Holy Spirit! He (or she) is always present with us. We do not have to feel or act weird to be assured of this. The Spirit is quietly present between us (the go-between God) in fellowship, especially in Holy Communion, or Mass, or in the sacraments like baptism. In tricky council meetings, the Spirit is in our decisions as our conscience. But preserve us from tongue speakers and excessively talkative dreamers! Deliver us from flighty flibbertigibbets! All that is unnerving and embarrassing. It's not the way we work out God's commission. Positively No.

These parts of the Body of Christ believe that the gift of prophecy is foundational. For at the beginning of Christianity, the Holy Spirit spoke in the great councils and creeds which nailed down the truths of the faith. And then throughout history, with church splits and the burgeoning of new denominations, the Spirit spoke in the doctrinal statements of faith.

From these first principles, it is now up to us to fathom the mind of God and the way ahead. We must act responsibly, partnering with the Lord in the mission in the world. Never forgetting that the Spirit speaks in the everyday through the Bible, which week by week teaches us from its treasures.

In some quarters, there are those who cherish holy women and men, prophets who have spoken for God in bygone years: mystics, monks, solitaries and spiritual writers. We know that contemporary life throws out outstanding gifts of visionary people, sometimes outspoken (Mother Theresa, Desmond Tutu). But surely these are the exception rather than the rule?

In the rare case of a false prophet, an exposé unmasks and ends the personality cult and demonstrates just how dangerous a thing it can be. We saw the ramifications of this in the extraordinary goings on in the Nine O'clock Service. What began as an enlightened, bold, prophetic vision for the clubbing night life in Sheffield, ended with a pileup of casualties. Strange teachings infiltrated that vision and, as prophets strayed from accountability, relationships went haywire and scandals evolved to hit the international press. Get down prophets!

In the hurly-burly, run-of-the-mill church life, when so-called prophetic persons are at large, it is our duty to contain them so as not to get out of hand. Hence the wisdom of the elders is as ice on fire. Wildness tamed. Everything in order. Of course, we believe that God speaks through someone with a word of guidance or encouragement. Is this prophecy? It does not seem wildly exciting, but matter of fact. Down to earth.

On the one hand, the mainstream is completely right. The Holy Spirit was most certainly at work in the creeds, councils and statements of faith and is always at work in the sacraments of the church and in Holy Scripture. Holy men and women point the way to a greater life and at times there are failures among them (we know that disciplining out of order prophets is the biblical way). On the other hand, we ought never to limit, suppress or confine the Holy Spirit to a denominational practice.

In the seventies, praying students at a university were completely gobsmacked when they took their atheist friend to a mission service at the cathedral. Not only was there a sung high mass with incense at a low altar moved right down the nave, plus singing in tongues, the laying on of hands for healing, but also an altar call, to which the said atheist responded in person, receiving Christ as Saviour in the presence of all.

Just because it suits us to contain the Third Person of the Trinity to our comfort zones, that does not mean that we can prevent the Spirit from breaking out in whichever way he chooses to revitalise and renew the face of the earth (and our denomination).

The question of renewal brings us to a third large force in the contemporary worldwide Church: the evangelical-charismatic-pentecostal stream, which is a rather strange hybrid that is partially sold out on prophecy. We will nickname this group the In-betweeners, the ones who can't quite make up their minds about prophecy.

SLIGHTLY SOLD OUT ON PROPHECY

The evangelical-charismatic-pentecostal track is a conglomerate of historic denominations affected by the Charismatic Renewal of the last sixty years. From the Greek word *charis,* meaning 'gift' or 'grace', we get the plural form, *charismata* meaning 'gifts' or 'graces'. This was an outpouring of the Spirit, rediscovered as both Gift of God and Giver of the gifts of God. This explosive spiritual phenomenon ignited God's people as the Holy Spirit poured out his fire into dried up bones, bathing and immersing local congregations in a holy cauldron of power. Entire church communities were set ablaze in an astonishingly short period of time, the gospel gained momentum, and day by day people came to know Jesus.

God opened his treasure chest, singled out the gifts and showered down their blessing to enliven his church. People stayed awake all night praying and praising in tongues and the gifts were exercised in freedom. There was much teaching on their usage and on everyone being empowered to minister and pray for others — for healing, deliverance and salvation. In this way, leadership was developed and exercised.

Inevitably, as all were encouraged to hear the Lord *for themselves*, not only through the preacher or teacher, there came an awakening to prophecy. The new awareness of the nudges of the Holy Spirit led to a focused attention on listening to one's dreams and allowing the Lord to guide through vision. Prophecy propelled fresh expressions of doing church and mission. Prophecy accelerated vocations to full-time ministry as young and old heard God's call.

The Renewal (as it became known) was a dynamic and life-giving injection into an enfeebled mainstream church (Roman Catholic, Protestant and Orthodox), touching evangelicals in the Protestant denominations and spawning new churches.

The Roman Catholic Church was especially open and receptive. In the Second Vatican Council (1962–65), Pope John Paul XXIII prayed for a 'New Pentecost.' In 1975, Pope Paul VI welcomed an international charismatic conference to Rome as 'a chance for the church.' In the noughties, the sixteen million Catholic charismatics were recognised as a strong wing of the global church and now have their own office and staff in Vatican City. Part of its work is an annual international Catholic charismatic conference, and in 2010 I was invited as a delegate to Bari.

I was quite taken aback when welcomed on to the platform and introduced as an Anglican Prophet from England, but also asked, nay commanded, to prophesy over a Forward in Faith Anglican Bishop (those who oppose women's ordination) and his wife — no holds barred there then! Needless to say, we had an excellent discussion over breakfast the following morning.

During the seventies, eighties and nineties, a good many church leaders felt a prophetic call to renew their denominations by staying *within* the structures. Others, the 'Come Out' people, felt led prophetically to abandon the old wineskin of institutionalised church. They were the house churches, networks and independent groups.

The 'Come Out' people tried to grapple with church decline by showing an entirely new way of being church. They often began with a great deal of prophetic fanfare and visionary fervour. Sometimes these fresh impulses did not last and there was a return to institution and hierarchical control. At other times, division within leadership was tumultuous, leading to hurt and unfortunate misunderstandings.

There was so much that was good in prophecy. Wise leaders were discerning, listening to prophecy, and somehow maintaining unity. Oftentimes, it was not handled in a mature way.

As all heard, or thought they heard, the voice of God commanding this or that thing, or this or that venture, decisions were made which sometimes brought pain or friction or disorder. Was it God, was it not? Was the mess God's upsetting of the temple furniture, or leadership misreading His signs? Was it rebellion in the ranks against godly leaders, or leaders rebelling any old how?

Although the In-betweeners had prophecy at their heart in the beginning, as time has gone on, and probably due to its unpredictable nature, the gift has been harnessed and controlled. Except in rare instances, where prophets are recognised and set apart for that specific task, there is usually only a nodding acceptance of those who have a 'word from the Lord.' Really, it is up to the leader of the church to hear God for direction and vision. Prophecy and prophetic people are mostly there to encourage, to *confirm* what the leadership believes is the way ahead, not to set new direction nor strategise for leadership.

The degree of difficulty in overcoming and resolving differences of opinion concerning the way ahead, is shown in a recent parish upheaval. Two prophets, one a lay person the other the ordained leader of the church. Usually the lay prophet was listened to and valued, but not this time, when there was no agreement. The leader's response: Oh no, you have not heard God. Under the weight of the leader's erroneous prejudiced deafness and an official enquiry, councillors resigned and the church collapsed, leaving some to pick up the pieces after the fallout.

Naturally, there are exceptions to the control of prophecy and when there is a full flowering of mature prophecy in churches and ministries, we may perceive a light touch, the dancing hand of God the Holy Spirit. It has been my delight to work with ordained ministers and folk of every denomination, who, in their desire to hear the Lord, have been generous to a fault in allowing prophecy and prophetic teams full reign: 'What is God saying to me, my church, my neighbourhood?' (clergy retreats); 'Let's hear what the Holy Spirit is saying to us this morning' (church services); 'What is the Lord saying to us as we look ahead? (staff team); 'We want to hear what God might be saying to us as a region' (ecumenical conference); 'We've been making prophetic declarations over the beach!' (residents of a seaside resort); 'We've been prayer walking our town centre for seven weeks' (local church leaders); 'I've put prophetic scriptures in the foundations of our new build' (praying Christian).

Yet often the gift of prophecy appears *not* to be at the centre of the gospel endeavour. The gravitational pull is to mission—by whatever means and whatever the cost. The work and effort in an organisation is put into marketing and getting the word out. These things are commendable. But surely first prize must be hearing the voice of the Spirit as the Lord of the harvest? It seems crazy to ignore the gift of prophecy and we do so at the risk of missing the boat. We should really contend for the mission of the Church by setting the gift of prophecy right at the centre of all we do.

QUESTIONS FOR FURTHER DISCUSSION

Does your church put prophecy first in the way of the Pentecostal Church? If so, does it strengthen the mission of the church?

Does your church sit lightly to prophecy, leaving it to other churches? In what way do you feel that the mission of your church could be strengthened by this gift?

Does your church have a take it or leave it approach to prophecy? What are the hindrances to the use of the gift of prophecy?

4

FREEING PROPHECY:
NO FEAR

Having ploughed through the previous chapter you would be forgiven for thinking, 'Help! Prophecy is a minefield, I must have missed the sign to Keep Out: Hidden Land Mines'. And to be sure, you would have a point. If the Church has bungled prophecy at times, and some individual Christians been off-putting, making a bit of a pig's ear out of the whole business (putting it bluntly), this forum is unlikely to attract the punters. More than likely it will be a magnet for the flaky few on the fringe.

Well then, if that's the case, it must be time to get back to basics, to the trusty Bible for what *it* says. The problem with this pithy solution is that different Church streams interpret the biblical verses on prophecy with their own *bias*. The same is true for other questions, too.

Take the prickly problem of women teaching or leading men (1 Tim 2:12). In some denominations, in the three streams we looked at in the last chapter, only male leaders and teachers are allowed; for other denominations, *that* idea is unbelievably old-fashioned and dated. Incidentally, this could go a long way to explaining the acceptance or non-acceptance of women who prophesy.

There is no blueprint for prophecy in the Bible. On the contrary, it can be dauntingly confusing. The Old Testament bristles with indignant prophets and their fabulous visions of God, on a roll about justice and sin. They seem to have barely anything to do with Jesus, whom the New Testament calls a prophet and lists ways in which prophecy fits into the life of the Church, but is a bit thin on detail. I suppose this explains why denominations make their own rules.

We could say that along the way we have missed the beauty of prophecy. Sometimes our expertise stands in the way of the raw materials and we have tamed and domesticated the lumpy sticky-out bits to fit our lifestyles and expectations. By so doing, we may have missed the explosive power of the biblical writings, which can be bombshells in our situations.

I write this in the aftermath of the awful Grenfell Tower fire, where many lost their lives and were critically injured. A baby was thrown from a window and people jumped from the tenth floor as over a hundred flats went up in a smouldering furnace in west London. What is the word on the street now? For the writers of the New Testament letters aimed their reflections at congregations very like our communities of faith today.

Those early Middle Eastern Christian communities (a mix of Jews, Greeks and

Romans) lived in a multifaith environment among variant pagan and religious faiths. A violent society with outbreaks of anti-Christian persecution, and an underground Church — secret Christians not unlike we in the West, afraid of breaking the taboo of political correctness and mentioning Jesus' name in public. It is to these people groups facing huge challenges to their belief in the gospel of Jesus Christ that the letters were written. We can read them as directed to us, too, in similar situations and needing to hear the word of the Lord.

Let us read these texts then as lively commentaries, in other words what church communities were *already* practising. Hopefully, we will have a window on their practices and something of their fearlessness toward prophecy may inspire us.

IMITATING THE EARLY CHURCH

Our first clue in this matter of imitating the early Jewish Christians is that they knew their *legacy*. They knew what they were worth. They stood on the shoulders of the giants of faith who had gone before them. They really did understand that the Hebrew prophets (Amos, Jeremiah, Joel, Isaiah etc.) spoke and wrote their messages of consolation, judgment or wisdom not into a vacuum, but into real situations at important historic moments. They were not blundering buffoons, idly ruminating on mountains about a god far removed from history. Far from it. They knew their call and the worth of their words. Their God was involved in the nitty gritty and in the destiny of the nation and the prophecies pulsate with purpose.

With this background, then, the New Testament urges believers to honour prophecies: 'Do not despise the words of prophets' (1 Thess 5:20). The belief that prophecy steers destinies was the Jewish inheritance; therefore, for a Christian, the greater the faith in that birthright the greater the trust in the gift of prophecy given 'in proportion to faith' (Rom 12:6). This clue tells us that the early Church *expected* the Lord to speak through prophecy. They were on the tiptoe of expectation waiting for Jesus to speak, hence the command to desire prophecy.

This Jesus, who longs to speak to his people and shepherd them, is our second clue to imitating the first Christians. God *pastors* his people. If we know what we are worth, the interest the Lord shows in our histories and destinies, then we will want to know what He is saying to us now. *Pastorally*, therefore, the gift of prophecy helps to point the way for the Church and for individuals.

A verse we have looked at before, 'strive for the spiritual gifts, and especially that you may prophesy' (1 Cor 14:1), was written to very busy Corinthian Christians. In fact, they were being busy all over the place in ungodly ways. Immorality and pagan religion were rife, and they were a disorderly bunch when it came to worship.

You would think that the last thing their founder Paul would encourage would be prophecy. Surely this would add yet another 'silly' dimension to the confusion? Apparently not. This verse is written, not as a statement of doctrinal belief, but as an instruction. The gift of prophecy is a way of acquiring wisdom for a congregation inundated with many pastoral concerns. It probably ought to be an integral part of our pastoral ministry today.

A woman testified on a prayer chain link to having heard God tell her to embark on a Jericho walk around her house. She obeyed, imitating Joshua. Every day for seven days she walked around her house praying and on the seventh day she walked around it seven times. Two weeks later, a terrible fire circled 360 degrees around her home, leaving it untouched but destroying eighteen others in the vicinity.

Moving from prophecies to prophets in the early Church, we come to a third clue, linked to the first two clues, which are *groups* of prophets. The legacy of Old Testament prophecy was a bunch of anointed prophets who tried to shepherd Israel (often unsuccessfully) by means of their words. We find this pattern in the early church. The Corinthian letters treat prophets as a distinct group. We know this from the statement, 'anyone who claims to be a prophet' (1 Cor 14:37), which is meaningless unless there was such a unique group. That there was such a group is evident from the foundational gifts appointed by the Lord and spelt out as 'first apostles, second prophets' (1 Cor 12:28). That these are people who hold some kind of recognised position in a community is plain from the question: 'Are all prophets? (1 Cor 12:29) These people would be local and integral to their community, staying put to keep an eye on the foundations of the local congregation.

A renewal venture in a rural part of the country has a small team of prophets and pastors, recognised by the vicar, which holds the reins to guide the infant vision through its teething problems. The Well meets once a month as part of the parish but with a unique call to worship; the team meets once a month to ensure that the vision is still on track.

A fourth clue to the practice of prophecy goes hand in hand with the idea of a group, and is the question of *authority*. From the Book of Acts, we learn that there is a set of leaders whose prophetic gift is authoritative: it is accepted as a

ministry to the Church. Among the circle visiting
the congregation in Antioch is Agabus who
predicts a famine (Acts 11:27, 28), Barnabas ('son
of prophecy' or 'son of encouragement') and
Paul, who never describes himself as a prophet
but as one who receives revelations from the
Lord (Acts 13:1-2; Gal. 1:12). When Agabus and
Paul meet on a separate occasion in Caesarea, the
prophet brings a dramatic warning. In a
symbolic action, he binds his own feet and hands
with Paul's belt, predicting that the owner of the
belt will be captured by the Jews and handed
over to the Gentiles (Acts 21:10-11). The
prophecy came true in Paul's imprisonment not
long after this event.

A large network of over eighty groups with
a common vision of local renewal and
evangelism, has as one of its core values
the gift of prophecy. At its annual
international conference, teams of
prophets from different cities who are
known to be authoritative, hold prophetic
appointments, giving vision, direction and
encouragement to the team leaders of
each group.

A fifth clue to prophecy in the primitive Church
is related to the group idea, and to the concept of
travelling or itinerant prophets. As we have seen,
there seem to have been prophets settled in

church communities, but then there were those who were unsettled and sent out from Antioch (Acts 13:1–2). Paul and the team were on the move, travelling from place to place on God's mission.

There is a great example of the ministry of these travelling prophets from the Didache or *Teaching of the Twelve Apostles* (most probably dating c.100 AD), which gives us a snapshot into what could have been the order and practice of the primitive Church. Boundaries are set: itinerant prophets are free to minister in a congregation for two days but if they overstay their welcome they are false prophets! Prophets speaking in the Spirit are not to be judged; however, not everyone who speaks in the Spirit is a prophet, but only if they hold to the ways of the Lord. Prophets teaching the truth, but not doing what they teach, are false prophets. Prophets demanding money or something else must not be listened to; only if requests for gifts are made for another's sake. These clear instructions show us that the leaders of early Christianity cast a gimlet eye upon prophesying, being on the lookout for heresies and enthusiasms, which leads us to another hint in our quest for biblical prophesying.

The sixth clue is the *discernment* to know what makes a prophecy truly of the Lord. At first glance, it is hard to tell what distinguishes the pagan Greek prophets (or Sybils) from Jewish prophesying, yet there are distinctions. These are the signs of the presence of Yahweh in Israel's prophets: they are God's mouthpiece; they speak inspired words not predetermined or logically thought out; these words are not teachings or ethical counsels but the very voice of God to disclose his will.

The Greek Sybils were prophetesses who delivered their words of enlightenment in raving ecstasies, but also as religious ethical instructions (a difference from the Hebrew prophets). The Sybil or sage was a teacher or a master to the pupil desiring wisdom (a difference). But she was aloof and isolated from the disciple, compared with the Hebrew prophets who identified with their people, living and working among them (a difference). How does all this relate to the New Testament instructions?

Converts from a Greek or Hellenistic background, jam-packed with magic and soothsayers, continued to live and work among pagan teachers and oracle-givers. Small wonder that they are told not to indulge in religious excitements; that they have but one master, Jesus; and that they are to become caring communities of love and power. Disciples are to concentrate on developing the Church in the ways of Jesus Christ.

Prophecy has an integral role to play in this mandate of building the Church. The word 'edification' is used over and over to discern prophetic utterance (see 1 Cor 14). When 'edification' is at work there are intelligible and instructive exhortations, urgings or persuasions which encourage and build up or edify the Body of Christ. Even an unbeliever may be convicted and converted by a chance hearing of prophecy. Here are the genuine signs that God is present in the prophesying.

> At a church weekend retreat at the sea, a reluctant husband, along for the entertainment and never the talks, unexpectedly appeared at the late evening's epilogue, during which there was a word in a tongue with an interpretation. So impressed was he by this direct speech, that his wife had a sleepless night answering his questions about the Lord, who was drawing him ever closer. Joy at the early morning prayers the next day!

A seventh and final clue to exercising prophecy is in the preaching or teaching of the *biblical text as prophecy*. When Peter preaches on the day of Pentecost, he digs deep into a prophecy from Joel 2, a passage he may well have been meditating upon for ten days in the upper room (see Acts 1–2). *This* outpouring of the Holy Spirit, he declares prophetically, is *that* which Joel prophesied. It is being fulfilled and coming true today! Thousands put their trust in Jesus following his sermon preached in the power of the Spirit.

Paul does an interesting thing to the Old Testament texts about water from the rock in the wilderness (Ex 17:5–7). He draws a parallel to Jesus Christ being that same rock from which water flows to quench our thirst (1 Cor 10). What can we learn from these two examples? That the early Church assumed that Scripture was prophecy and that the Holy Spirit was always at work igniting and inspiring the text to reveal fresh meanings.

Seven clues (not exhaustive of course) to the New Testament practice of prophesying. That's all good, we may respond, but how will these ways be *activated*? How does the gift of prophecy fit into the structures of church? This question must surely lead us to an active investment in the fivefold pattern of ministry.

INVESTING IN THE FIVEFOLD PATTERN

There is only one reference in Scripture to the fivefold pattern, but this important passage shows us how a network of training and equipping the saints for the work of ministry can help leaders to implement best practice for prophesying:

> The gifts he [Christ] gave were that some would be apostles, some prophets, some evangelists, some pastors and teachers, to equip the saints for the work of ministry, for building up the body of Christ.
> **Ephesians 4:11–12**

Remember the study of Word and Spirit – the two hands of God – in a previous chapter? Now imagine the hand of Christ, where each finger represents one of the five gifts of *people*: apostle, prophet, evangelist, teacher and pastor. This is a five-finger exercise and the Lord holds the score. With each gift perfectly coordinated, he orchestrates the symphony of Church, conducting it into its fullest potential and coaxing from it its most awesome sound.

In this way, the Body matures from childish ways until it is grown up in Christ, as the passage continues:

> We must no longer be children, tossed to and fro and blown about by every wind of doctrine, by people's trickery, by their craftiness in deceitful scheming. But speaking the truth in love, we must grow up in every way into him who is the head, into Christ, from whom the whole body, joined and knit together by every ligament with which it is equipped, as each part is working properly, promotes the body's growth in building itself up in love.
> **Ephesians 4: 14–16**

Just as a hand is incapacitated when one of its fingers is injured or missing, so the Christian mission is weakened by a non-existent or wounded ministry. We must try to keep the 'finger' of prophecy free from injury, active and fully functioning. We have seen the importance of prophets, second only to apostles in God's order for organizing the Church (1 Cor 12:28). These are the two 'beginner' gifts. They are the people who begin churches, who start-up congregations with vision for the mission. However, to get maximum mileage out of the gift, there can never be one person only or just a few people who do all the work. The purpose of the fivefold ministry is always to empower *others*, to 'equip the *saints* for the work of ministry' (Eph 4:12). That's you and I, every Joe, every member, every Christian.

This simple idea of empowering others has generated countless books and manuals from strong denominational positions. These stances swing from one extreme, that only very select people are called to be an important Apostle or Evangelist, etc. (capitalised to show their 'office'), to the other extreme, that every single member of the Body is called to function in just one of the five gifts most of the time. We will go with a middle path somewhere between 'everyone is called to be one or the other' and 'only a handful are called to be one or the other.' Let it be said that none of the four observations is theoretical. In my 'hands on' experience in churches and networks, I have observed each practised successfully.

Firstly, we will be concerned with teaching that anyone can prophesy, as it is the Spirit who distributes the gift as he pleases. However, this is strictly on an 'as and when' basis—as the Spirit wishes and when the gift is given to someone.

The gift is not 'owned' by the person, it comes and goes depending on the moment of opportunity. The function of the fivefold scheme is to enable this to happen more and more frequently in small and big meetings, the teacher or pastor giving space and time for the Holy Spirit to interrupt, to nudge, to speak through others.

At a New Year's Eve Prayer Party at a large London church filled to capacity, there came a moment when prophecy was invited and two or three spoke to a gathering from the four corners of the globe, words of encouragement for the coming year.

Secondly, usually there will be folk who are gifted with prophecy more often than others. They begin to stick out whenever a congregation meets to pray or worship as being accurate in their messages and anointed by the Holy Spirit. They could continue doing this ad infinitum (gaining a little platform for themselves) or they could be usefully employed to raise the bar in the church by raising up others in the gift of prophecy.

Equipping others is the harder option as it requires sacrifice and commitment on the part of the prophetic leaders and the learners. The art of passing on 'kitchen secrets' to budding prophets is a skill to nurture and practise. Multiplication of prophetic gifting (as the Spirit directs of course), especially inter-generationally, will spread the load of prophesying, encouraging both young and old, as the prophet foretold (see Joel 2:28–29). Broadening the base of prophetic people is *the* essential brick in building prophecy in the church.

A lay leader at a large church, especially gifted in prophetic teaching, gathered around herself a small group each week and taught them how to hear the 'now' word from Scripture, the word pertinent to the people at that time. After a while these women felt confident to teach others and thus prophetic teaching was multiplied.

Thirdly, at some point leadership may feel that the person doing the equipping and raising up others is truly part of the fivefold ministry. It may even be time (crazy idea!) to invite him or her on to the leadership team. To baulk at this idea is not very scriptural. We have seen that the New Testament practice is to recognise prophets as a distinct group in congregations and the travelling ministry. And in *some cases,* they were leaders, plainly a gift of the Spirit to which not all are called. But when a prophet *is called* to be a leader and leads diligently (see Rom 12:8), the benefits for all can be out of this world!

A small community church had on its team those who had worked closely together in the past. They finally plucked up the courage to enlarge the team, inviting on to it a very pastoral prophet, someone who had the heart of the people but also the vision of God. A great success!

Fourthly, the practice of the fivefold ministry can be extended to cities, towns, villages, even nations. Prophets begin to network with other prophets in an area, praying and seeking God for wisdom and divine strategies. These can be extremely influential groups for breakthroughs in the church's mission.

An online early morning Prophetic Prayer Watch has eighty participants (and growing), from around the UK. As they pray together in cyberspace, often not known to one another, they stand for the nation and for God, to hear Him and to hold back the tide of evil—a remarkable work. Some participants in the prayer watch hold influential positions and speak on behalf of God to MPs or those in local government.

This short journey into the New Testament texts has given us some signposts to the practice of prophecy. There is one further step to take before we can leave the topic of freeing up prophecy, and it is to do with being a friend of God — a good biblical prophetic principle. Abraham was a friend of God and Moses spoke 'mouth to mouth' with Yahweh. The Lord God 'does nothing, without revealing his secret to his servants the prophets' (Amos 3:7).

INTIMACY WITH JESUS CHRIST

The Bible begins with a divine conversation in the heart of the Trinity: 'Let us make a human being in our image.' Then the conversation moves out toward the human being created. God and Adam walk together in the cool of the day. What conversations! Walking and talking with God your Creator. A pleasure, a joy. And then: pain and agony in sin's separation. Yearning, our hand reaching out and God's endearing enduring, so wonderfully depicted by Michelangelo on the ceiling of the Sistine Chapel in Rome — the divine hand outstretched yet … not connecting. Yet … transparent is the Father's love for the fallen race of Adam in the broken hands of Jesus fixed to the cross. The pinned hands drawing us back to the divine heart to enfold us in love.

Our desire for intimacy is as nothing compared with God's desire for heart-to-heart communion with his creatures. He longs to speak with us, as at the beginning of creation, to reveal his heart, his mind, his ways. In Jesus Christ, this holy conversation again becomes a reality.

On earth, Jesus walked and talked with his disciples, opening his heart to them in his joys and trials. After his crucifixion and resurrection, he opened the Hebrew scriptures to them, showing them the things concerning himself, how the former writings, the prophets and psalms had foreshadowed his incarnation, death and resurrection.

Jesus Christ is the opener of Scripture and the key to both Testaments. Since his ascension, Jesus is seated at the right hand of the Father, but the chair from which he teaches is the cross and our classroom is the place where we contemplate the cross. Therefore, to know the thoughts and intentions of Jesus' heart – as he knows ours – means to desire his friendship, to draw near to Jesus, to lean on his chest (as John the Beloved Disciple). These were the beliefs dear to the Fathers of the early Church.

To sit at the feet of the Lord is to come to a knowledge of ourselves: what makes us tick, what makes us get up in the morning and what gives us life. We also come to a knowledge of his word: 'Morning by morning he wakens, he wakens my ear to hear as those who are taught' (Isa 50:4). Here is the beginning of all prophecy. We may imitate the early Church and invest in the fivefold pattern, but *none* of this is of lasting value unless we enjoy an intimate friendship with the Lover of our souls. All prophetic activity is utterly useless, a sounding gong and a clanging bell unless it is birthed and covered in love. This starts in the inner sanctum of the heart.

QUESTIONS FOR FURTHER DISCUSSION

Do you find the idea of prophetic wisdom in pastoral work daunting or exciting? How could prophecy be incorporated into the day-to-day work of ministry?

Does the thought of an investment in the fivefold ministry give you the heebie-jeebies? If not, what steps could be taken to introduce this notion to the church or network or organisation?

How is your prayer life?

5

FAST-TRACKING PROPHECY: NO PROFESSIONALS

One could argue that the church can conduct its mission successfully without the slightest trace of any prophesying at all. After all, we have the Gospel and our task is to proclaim and live it. What difference will prophecy make? It will give us God's thoughts and plans. The raison d'être of this book (at the risk of being tedious and repetitive) is to show that our mission will have a sharp edge when the practice of robust prophesying is to the fore and not just an afterthought. Our constant prayer should be the ancient prayer of the Church, 'Come Holy Spirit.' He is the hand in the glove without which our efforts are useless.

If we concentrate our attention on being and becoming a prophetic Church, where all can prophesy as and when the Holy Spirit directs, we had better watch out! For the Spirit operates with fluidity and distributes his gifts as he wills and they can land on anyone at any time (1 Cor 12:11).

Does this mean that I need to be 'charismatic' to prophesy? Well, yes, whatever we may call the infilling of the Holy Spirit, we do need to ask and go on asking to be saturated and overflowing with the Holy Spirit. We need his power and a large part of the Spirit's power pack are the revelatory gifts which go together: tongues and interpretation, knowledge and wisdom, and prophecy.

With this in mind, then, how to speed up prophecy today? The short answer is that we abolish the idea that only 'professional' prophets (conference speakers, people with websites and blogs) can, and may prophesy. We should also lose the rather prejudiced caricature that prophets are found only in Africa or North America, and that usually they are out for financial gain. As we think about the *way* in which we prophesy, we have first to overcome the hurdle of *why* we, ordinary Christians, don't or won't prophesy.

ALL CAN PROPHESY

We left the previous chapter contemplating a sitting position at the feet of the Lord, adoring him, worshipping him and listening to his word. We can, however, go on sitting and loving and adoring and never *get up* to *go* with the word of the Lord. Someone with a sedentary 'couch potato' lifestyle, always sitting and never walking terribly far if it can be helped, will find that gradually those muscles used for walking will weaken and become more and more flabby with disuse. If it's true for the body, it's true for the soul.

An unexercised prophetic muscle will atrophy and waste away, ceasing to function. Or to use another analogy: the well of prophecy may dry up completely without intentional and regular filling. This would be a serious predicament. Surely, we do not wish to be a generation where, in the words of the prophet Amos, 'there is a famine on the land; not a famine of bread, or a thirst for water, but of hearing the words of the Lord' (8:11)?

But closer to home, and more personally than these high ideals, is the worry that we might get it wrong. So we are more than happy for the upfront people to go ahead, leaving it up to others more 'qualified', or to the one who looks like a prophet and the one *they* (meaning leadership) listen to. We say: 'I never get words and pictures like so-and-so', 'I'm not one for hearing God,' or 'I'm not called to be a prophet.'

Learning to prophesy is like a toddler learning to walk. We laugh delightedly at their tumbles, at their attempts to get up, at their courage. We love to see them going for it, fat little legs determinedly taking them across the room, and to the goal—the glass of water on the table just within reach. But the environment is safe for the toddler and can be safe for learners of prophecy. A place where we can use the muscle, get up, get moving and give it a go. And if we take a tumble and get it wrong, a loving family will help us up and teach us to learn from that mistake, from that little escapade. A condemning family will tell us that we are never to do that again, that we are an embarrassment to the family name and a hazard to the community. We may never walk again after that.

ALL CAN LEARN TO PROPHESY

Warming acknowledgment from others *is* wonderful, but if human beings are unsupportive, there is nothing to stop us from positioning ourselves before the Lord to hear from him for our own lives and for others. This is the first leg of the prophetic journey. The second leg, getting the word down in writing or speaking it out (prophecy is not prophecy until it is communicated), will be explored in the final chapter. First, however, we must learn to listen like a watchman at his post:

> I will stand at my watchpost,
> and station myself on the rampart;
> I will keep watch to see what he will say to me,
> and what he will answer concerning my complaint.
> **Habakkuk 2: 1**

Generally, I feel that less energy is spent on spiritual exercises than on physical exertions. I am amused at myself when I leap out of bed at the sound of the bin collection lorry to put out my forgotten bin. No problem in getting out early on a freezing icy morning to try out my new running trainers. Up with the larks as the sun's bright and a perfect day for a spring clean. Or on a fitness regime for the summer holidays and bike rides in the evening. I can spend more time preparing meals than I do in receiving spiritual daily bread. We are going against our natural desires when we set the alarm and get out of bed twenty minutes earlier than usual to pray, or delay putting out the light at night before we've read and prayed.

A prayerful position is first and foremost an intentional decision, birthed and cultivated in private struggle, until it becomes second nature to us. We will have to push back the clamouring demands and carve out space for this time. Other stuff will crowd in, demanding our attention. We will not feel like it, we will try it and abandon it when it doesn't appear to be working and we hear and see absolutely nothing. And we will be in good company. Elijah waited in his cave for an extremely long time (probably days) for the full play of natural elements: strong winds, an earthquake, a fire. Finally, when the tumults had ceased, there came the sound of a small silence. And God spoke (see 1 Kings 19).

I once heard a statement which has stuck with me: Demonstrate what you think of God by the quality of the time you give Him. Food for thought. We do need time for the Holy Spirit to settle upon us, to overshadow us like Mary, to 'impregnate' us with the word (Luke 1:35). And when the word of the Lord finally comes, what does it look like?

Here is a visual exercise to help us to recognise prophecy and, hopefully, to grow in the gift. It requires a bit of a stretch of the imagination. Let us imagine a tall ladder propped against a tree or a building or on a roof. Unless you are an agile athlete or a wall runner, the normal way up is to start at the bottom and proceed to climb rung by rung. The ladder progresses from the earth upwards, as did the ladder in Jacob's vision which was set on the earth and passed through to the heavens. The angels ascended and descended on this ladder (Gen 28:12). Our desire is to position a ladder upwards, from ourselves, so to speak, from the inner sanctuary of our hearts, to the Lord. We are spiritual athletes, exercising those spiritual eye and ear muscles as we learn to hear and see God.

The first rung of our ladder is Scripture. Methodically read a few verses each day. Sometimes the reading is uninspiring; at other times a word, a phrase or a sentence will seem to leap out with particular clarity, challenge or comfort. Begin to think deeply, to ponder this thought, to meditate and chew over it until it rings in your spirit and works its influence to change and shape. After a while you may find yourself sharing this word with another person and it becomes prophecy for them. The word may even travel further afield, as you share it with a church congregation or a mission group or a nation.

An example of a text which might be used more widely is Jeremiah 29:11: 'For surely I know the plans I have for you, says the Lord, plans for your welfare and not for harm, to give you a future with hope.' This verse, which begins as a personal word of encouragement, becomes prophetic when, anointed by the Spirit, it is shared more widely.

Up the ladder on to the next rung. While at prayer a sequence of words flits lightly through the mind like a fragile butterfly in flight. Try to hold them. These words are divine communications and usually come unsummoned by us. For example, 'I love you more than you know,' or 'I died for you, for *you*. Do you know how much I love you,' or 'Look to me and the shadow of your burden will fall behind you.' The Lord is speaking his comfort and assurance, and, although these sentiments are not direct quotations from the Bible, mostly they will echo Scripture. Google the word or phrase in Bible Gateway and be inspired by the number of references. Write them down. Write down the words God spoke.

Climb on to the rung above and find yourself in good company with many of the Lord's people. Have you been to a church service, meeting or conference where it is *that* song which gets everyone going? Songs can be an expression of the work of the Spirit in people's hearts and last for a season (months, even years). What is remarkable is the *same* song, loved and sung all over the world in different languages — a corporate witness in our spirits to prophetic lyrics inspired by the Spirit. There is no point in mentioning which songs have that effect because, by the time this book goes to print, the song with its prophetical message will have changed as the season has changed.

Going up the ladder we begin to mature in prophecy — not for the fainthearted. We are waiting to hear a message for someone else and this requires diligent effort. We must be patient in prayer and spiritually alert. Words, unlikely in an audible voice (but not impossible), are impressed upon the listener. There is a sense that the Spirit is speaking to bypass the mind, lifting the communication beyond what I would naturally think.

Recording, by writing down the communiqué, as it is being given, is essential. This prevents later embellishments and additions as we strive to give away what has been received. The length of the prophecy may be anything from a single word or sentence to a paragraph or pages of script. A warning: Length is not a sign of greater spiritual elevation. A short word of accurate prediction is of more prophetic worth than a rambling jumble of words and scriptures. And a provocation: Stretch that lazy muscle and don't be content with a single word: what else, is there more, what does it mean?

The next rung on the ladder is waiting and watching for what we may *see* in the Spirit. Pictures and images carrying messages from the Lord are granted as we pray. And even without prayer, as we go about our daily business. That is, these may occur naturally or supernaturally as prophetic signs to show us what God is up to.

A vivid illustration of just such a natural sign is in the Book of Jeremiah. The Lord gives an intriguing instruction: 'Come, go down to the potter's house, and there I will let you hear my words.' Jeremiah does exactly that and finds the potter busily working the clay. As he watches he sees the vessel ruined on the wheel but observes how the potter, nothing daunted, uses the same clay to reshape it. The Lord uses the craftsman's enterprise to point up Israel's brokenness on the wheel of the exile and the nation's return and restoration in the rebuilding. This same spoilt clay will become beautiful again (Jer. 18:1–11).

That passage is an example of a prophetic parable, that is, a story with a spiritual meaning giving hope for the future, in this case. The prophecy depends on sight and sound: the prophet's powers of observation and the attentiveness to hear the interpretation. In a low-key kind of way, we can become accustomed to God speaking to us through day-to-day, mundane situations. Quite often in recent years, I have noticed a correlation between plumbing problems in homes or buildings and spiritual issues in the inhabitants of these establishments, or in their domestic or work circumstances. In other words, the timing of plumbing breakdowns in the natural seem to coincide with spiritual states. It's time to take stock. Scripture even backs this up!

> For my people have committed two evils:
> they have forsaken me,
> the fountain of living water,
> and dug out cisterns for themselves,
> cracked cisterns
> that can hold no water
> **Jeremiah 2:13**

A woman walking to work in smart shoes gets a message from God. She sees a chap in a hoodie walking very quickly past in trendy trainers. She thinks, Hmm a young 'un on the go! To her great surprise, he turns out to be not so young! She realises that God is speaking to her about the right gear for the fast track in her life. Get with it, get going! Prophecy is for all ages.

Our senses tune in to creation for signs: a tree shedding its summer blazer is suddenly emblazoned in autumnal splendour. We realise that we, too, are entering a new season. What is God saying to us in this natural event? A fox pokes its head through a gap in the fence, an urban audacious fox. Cunning. A few hours later there is a sly twist in the tale in that situation at work and, caught unawares, I'm reminded of the text: 'Catch us the foxes, the little foxes, that ruin the vineyards—for our vineyards are in blossom' (Songs 2:15). God sent a warning bell.

Still on the same rung of the ladder of prophecy – what we *see* in the Spirit – but moving from seeing naturally to seeing supernaturally. Some may find this too much like hard work, a strain on the brain to force one's mind to lie fallow and useless while one's spirit has free reign. If we study the Bible, however, we shall discover heaven breaking into the lives of people in various states of wakefulness or sleep. They are our models as we pursue this topic.

Consider Isaiah, a priest serving fully awake in the Temple, suddenly caught up in a magnificent vision of the holiness of the Lord God Almighty. There is sight and sound. Angels call out to one another; a live coal purges his lips and the prophet responds in repentance for his country (Isaiah 6). Think about Daniel, sound asleep in Babylon, visited by dreams and visions of the night: political scenarios telling of what is yet to come in the life of the king, and previews into the future realties of surrounding nations (Dan 7). In the midst of a sorrowful life in exile, away from home, Ezekiel has a window on heaven thrown wide open and is shown the glory of God in panoramic vista: the moving throne of God and the four living creatures (Ez 1).

And, lest we think that vision is passé, consider an eighty-two-year-old woman, widowed in her twenties, who, sixty years ago, as she stood at her window, saw a vision which was completely physical, the Lord Jesus coming on the clouds. She was so terrified that she ran to her bed and buried her head in a pillow. Twenty years later she became a Christian. She treasures this vision and it motivates her mission to reach out for lost souls. He *is* coming again!

We hear today of many, many Muslims who are seeing Jesus in vision and dreaming about Jesus and coming to faith in Jesus. For the arena of prophecy is also the stuff of dreams, in which the subconscious is acutely sharpened to receive God's messages. One example among numerous stories is Joseph. At the conception and birth of Jesus, dreams come as comfort (Matt 1:20–21), a warning, (Matt 2:13) and guidance (Matt 2:20).

A school teacher had a warning dream of a difficult boy in her classroom, defying her authority. It happened exactly as predicted but she knew what to do because she had been warned and the unruly lad was brought to order with a new authority.

Keep standing on this rung and nurture a love of the Lord's presence. As we exercise an awareness of his presence we may be surprised to feel tangibly his dear self with us. We may feel the touch of his hand, even smell his fragrance and taste his word like honey in the mouth. On this rung, our visions may include light and sound: rushing waters, trumpets, heavenly music, angelic song, colours or luminosity — God's audio-visual features in the treasure chest of prophecy. A step too far? Why not? Listen.

NOT ALL ARE PROPHETS

Really? What's that about? We've just said that all can prophesy. Actually, it's a relief to know that not all are called to be prophets. That would be an overload of the highest order. The Church needs balance and all the gifts of people to fulfil its mission, as we discovered in the fivefold ministry in the previous chapter. Anyhow, as a friend once pointed out crisply, the prophets had such a tough time, who would want to be one? Yet there *are* prophets and the Church ought to learn how to discern the gift.

When all things are working perfectly together, a community with its leadership may begin to detect that so-and-so seems to hear from God very accurately. Leaders take her e-mails seriously. When she speaks out in a gathering people sense the Lord in the message. The principle is: 'Let two or three prophets speak, and let the others weigh what is said' (1 Cor 14:29). As the prophecies are weighed and tested to be found true, and as time goes by, this person will earn the trust of the local church, until he or she becomes recognisably more prophetic than most and could be said to be a prophet, if that seemed the guiding of the Lord.

What about these more-prophetic-than-most people themselves? How do they feel? How do they respond to this testing? They need to be sure of their call but not overly confident either. It's no good going around saying, 'I'm a prophet.' That's not how it works.

Prophets are recognised through a discernment process in the local situation. And what if they are not? What if they are hated, rejected and overlooked, constantly? We will look at the reasons for this more closely in the final chapter. For the moment, suffice to give a few pointers as to what makes someone feel that they are more prophetic than most.

For these people, there is a close relationship with Jesus Christ and an acknowledgment that all prophecy depends upon the Holy Spirit and not human thought. Often in prayer there is a clear sense of what God is saying personally and sometimes there is a word for the church community—a specific instruction for the way ahead, vision for the future, or a warning about a course of action, for example. At other times, when at prayer on behalf of others – standing in the gap for their situations – there is a keen awareness of a solution or a plan for them. An anointing to prophesy manifests in a tangible 'weightiness' or, conversely, a feeling of weakness and loss of strength. Or there is a sensation of heat or burning in the stomach area or the top of the head. Or else there is no physical impression at all except an inner conviction that won't go away, of the burden of the word of the Lord. And at other times there are no clues whatsoever, apart from the knowledge that not to share this word would be disobedience.

> If I say, 'I will not mention him,
> or speak any more in his name,'
> then within me there is something like a burning fire
> shut up in my bones;
> I am weary with holding it in,
> and I cannot.
> **Jeremiah 20:9**

Does being an extra prophetic person mean I must be full-time? Not really, unless you live on a desert island or in a cave or hermit's cell. Even in our day, there are ones called to solitude and set apart to read the times and to pray for our turbulent age. Thank God for nuns and monks, and others who stand and pray as watchman on our city walls. We have no idea of the effect of their prayers.

However, for those who hold down taxing jobs, tend to family concerns, and work for local church or community, retreat is not an option. More than likely, the word of God will come on the coalface and in the heat of the everyday, as strategies and game plans are pursued in prayer. In the market place, prophets can be change agents of God's grace, offering assessments and solutions to benefit communities. The same applies to prophets in the arts, entertainment industry, education, politics, sport, finance and the media. Heavenly plans infiltrated into these secular settings can only be exciting.

In the centre of a city, inside its medieval walls, lives someone with civic responsibility and a passion to hear God for the ancient town. Down below in her basement is a 'war room', its walls covered with prayers, prophetic declarations and maps. She and her friends are fighting a spiritual war, and prevailing. As part of the wider strategy for the area they are seeing results in the life of the community as the Gospel of Jesus reaches out to overcome social neglect and deprivation and people are won for Christ.

Prophetic vision and the spiritual stamina to see it through: Do we have this in our day as the odds mount up against the truth of Jesus?

In another ancient city stands a house in the cathedral close, dedicated as a watch tower of prayer. On every level of the abode there are prayers and promises, visions and dreams posted and pasted on the walls. A 24/7 cauldron of holy fire, greater than enemy fire—the prayers of the saints.

If we observe at least some of the principles set out above, we will probably be less likely to experience haphazard or untrustworthy prophesying. Come to think of it, most of our reluctance to embrace the gift is because we have heard, not *false* prophecy exactly, but that which is slightly wacky and off-the-wall and delivered by weirdo's.

Perhaps we might have thought that John the Baptist belonged to this category: what he said was hard-hitting and my goodness, what a zany guy from another planet. It wasn't false; just difficult to receive. But because his words are enshrined in Scripture, that makes them alright. How about others who seem a bit like this, in the flesh? Are they true or muddled messengers? This is where we must turn to safeguarding the Church against flaky prophets, the subject of the last chapter.

QUESTIONS FOR FURTHER DISCUSSION

Does the idea that anyone can prophesy elate you or confuse you or terrify you or humble you?

Have you ever tried to ascend a ladder of prophecy? If so, at which rung have you stuck?

Are you one of those more prophetic than most, or do you recognise those who are? Do you trust yourself or them?

6

FACING THE FUTURE:
NO FLAKINESS

In this chapter, we will try to tie up loose ends. These ends are complex and somewhat intertwined. How to communicate prophecy and how to relate to prophets. It's a chicken and egg story. Which comes first: communicating the prophecy well, or the relationship between the prophet and the recipient? Both are essential and yet not always possible to achieve at the same time.

In church settings, the way in which prophecy is communicated is vital, yet a wholesome relationship between the prophet and the rest of the team is life-giving. Sadly, in both these areas, churches are found lacking in the skills required to bolster and advance the prophetic gift. If we can get it right, much of the eccentric and erratic flakiness found in prophecy might disappear. For the sake of continuity with the previous chapter, we will begin with the question of communicating the word of the Lord.

PROPHECY AND COMMUNICATION

Then the Lord answered me and said:
Write the vision;
make it plain on tablets,
so that a runner may read it.
Habakkuk 2:2

In the previous chapter, we dealt with the first leg of the prophetic journey: tactical ways of sharpening up to hear and see God in prayer and in daily life. In this, the final chapter, our project is to get that second leg over the prophetic hurdle: the struggle to share what we see and hear. It is completely pointless having boxes of undelivered prophetic words under the bed, or in filing cabinets, however neatly stashed and dated. Unless these words and pictures are *communicated* they cannot be called prophecies in the truest sense, since they are dated and totally useless.

On this point, there is something to be learned from the sign of the loincloth which the prophet is ordered to buy, put around his waist and then take off and hide in the cleft of a rock. Naturally, after many days the cloth is ruined and useless. In the same way, Israel was made to cling to the Lord but had chosen to go off after other gods, so that it fell out of fellowship with him (Jer 13:1-11). Similarly, a prophetic word fashioned in intimacy with God (the loincloth clinging to the waist), but then squirreled away conveniently out of sight (hidden in the cleft of the rock), will lose its impact and be of no use to anyone.

This principle applies to scrapping old prophecies which have passed their sell-by date. They cannot be dredged up again to apply to a new situation. Either they will have been fulfilled, thus accomplishing their purpose, or their fulfilment delayed through disobedience, until finally, out of step with divine time, the prophecy lies abandoned. An example of this is a warning in Scripture linked to healing:

> He said, "If you will listen carefully to the voice of the Lord your God, and do what is right in his sight, and give heed to his commandments and keep all his statutes, I will not bring upon you any of the diseases that I brought upon the Egyptians; for I am the Lord who heals you.
> **Exodus 15:26**

There is a conditional clause in the prophecy: 'If you will obey [paraphrase]'. The condition of healing is obedience to the laws of God. A church, for example, which has experienced a repeated pattern of serious illness and death among its leadership, should examine itself and repent. It could be that healing is being delayed through straying from God's commands or disobedience or by an attack of Satan (like Job).

The whole reason for prophecy is to build up the Body of Christ. The sooner we learn how to deliver the message the better for the church community. The easiest method is to record in writing immediately we receive the word, even while we are praying, as we tend to forget later. This could be in a notebook or journal, on a phone or computer. We may even choose to record it audibly on a mobile or dictaphone. However we choose to log the prophetic word, the main thing is that we show the Lord our willingness to have it used in whichever way he pleases. We pray, commit it to him and wait for his timing to see it delivered.

When the Lord gives us the nod, so to speak, we give the message by e-mail, letter or note, to the person concerned. In written form, the prophecy is easy to read at leisure. Once it is surrendered, our work has ended. There is no need to fret and fume if there is a lack of response. Our job is done; it is now up to God. If the word is ignored or, even worse, rejected, we may be tempted to throw our toys out of the cot: 'That's it, I'll never try again.' Don't do that! Instead, get up, dust off and go back to the watch tower. Oh, and forgive — very important.

When it comes to an ordinary person who is not a leader having a word or picture for the encouragement of a meeting or church service, either beforehand or in the middle of the worship, what to do then? A good procedure is a written note to those responsible for leading; even better to a prophetic person in leadership. Discerning leaders will welcome these offerings as a basket of summer fruit, ripe and ready to be given out. Bad fruit will, of course, not be handed out—that's the gift of discernment used wisely.

There are, however, often complications in what appears to be a straightforward practice. There is the awkward moment when, in the middle of proceedings, someone feels inspired with a prophetic word and plucks up the courage to go up to the front with this good piece of ripe summer fruit. The leader listens to the word but does nothing with it and no-one ever refers to it. One can only surmise that it is an interruption the leader feels the service can do without.

Getting over the hurdle of rejection and moving on can prove even more complicated than bringing the word. The messenger may leave the building angrily and vow never to return: others get the chance to speak, but never me; I'm not part of the inner circle; I feel on the fringe. The issue becomes bigger and bigger in the mind and the sore place becomes a festering wound, carried around from church to church and affecting adversely the work of prophecy.

For healing to come, it is so important that there is a grown-up spiritual response. The anger or hurt taken to Jesus; a forgiving heart; no gossip; the predicament explained to an unbiased friend or someone in leadership; and an ongoing openness to prophesying again, of course!

We must now tackle the tricky question of prophecies which cannot be written down ahead of time but pour forth verbally as an uninterrupted stream of inspiration on the spot. Why tricky? The short answer is that their content is not always known in advance and this is uncomfortable for some. However, the evidence for this proverbial hot potato in action is in Scripture — loud and clear:

> Let two or three prophets speak, and let the others weigh what is said. If a revelation is made to someone else sitting nearby, let the first person be silent. For you can all prophesy one by one, so that all may learn and all be encouraged.
> **1 Corinthians 14:29–31**

This passage gives a small glimpse into disciplined freedom: two or three prophecies allow time to judge what is spoken; overabundant prophesying brings indigestion, i.e. a group cannot absorb too much at once; a single person should not monopolise the prophesying but move over to allow another to speak.

How might we action this model? Best practice is a discerning leader who will allow two or three people the microphone so that the messages may be spoken freely. If the words are genuinely of the Lord, they will take wings and do their work without human aid. However, a leader may act as interpreter for the benefit of the congregation who may wish to receive prayer in response to the prophecy.

Such prophesying may well lead to worship, glorifying God, or to repentance and to a prophetic action of some sort. For example, if forgiveness was the gist of the message, people could be encouraged to respond by kneeling at the cross, or by going forward for prayer, or walking across the room to a brother or sister to seek reconciliation. An outworking of the prophecy in a practical manner can be very helpful indeed.

Spontaneous prophecies are the most difficult both to deliver and to decipher, as our discipleship doesn't seem to cover this aspect of prophesying and it often shows signs of immaturity. Someone speaks, and in the middle of the muddle of personal reflection and sermonising there is a nugget of truth. The one genuine article from the Lord is embellished with thoughts and prayers running through the mind at the time. I've done this myself and have wondered whether the New Testament principle in textual criticism should be a prophetic tool too: *brevior et difficilior*, the shorter and more difficult the reading, the more trustworthy.

How to record prophecies which are spoken spontaneously? An alert sound technician recording the sermon will not switch off when a prophecy is being given but will keep the recording going for future reference. It is a common practice in forward thinking churches for people receiving personal prophecies to record these on their mobile phones. They can be taken away and prayerfully considered.

PROPHECY AND LEADERSHIP

In three decades of working as a prophetic leader on church staff teams, lecturing in theological colleges and teaching both ministers and lay people of all denominations on retreats and conferences, I have observed a common dynamic. I offer these comments tentatively, realising that they will be incomplete and probably not universal. The nub of the matter is that there is very often a disconnect between people with prophetic gifts and leadership. It usually has to do with issues of control.

There are probably a few reasons for the reluctance to welcome prophets. One could be that the minister, vicar or priest has seen some flaky behaviour and finds prophetic people off-putting and untrustworthy. Or that he or she is unused to prophets, not quite sure what to do with them and keeps them at arm's length.

Another reason could be that a church has a vision statement, and knows exactly where it wants to go and so doesn't want further input from prophets: 'When we need a prophet, we will call them! And when we do, they will probably confirm what we already know because we have heard the Lord.' For these reasons, and, I'm quite sure, for many more, prophets are avoided.

Now I know the stock phrases: prophets are never popular; John the Baptist was beheaded and Elijah called the troubler of Israel. This doesn't wash when it comes to the early histories: biblical evangelists were not popular all the time; most of the original Twelve were martyred; writers and apologists were beheaded.

The early Christians did not play it safe, whether they were prophets or not, and they paid the price. And yet they were a *team*. They needed one another. They needed the gifts of one another for the mission to be strong. To make way for prophets on team is the same as giving leeway to pastors and teachers, to evangelists and apostles. For this reason, therefore, an investment in relationship between prophets and leaders should be made for the sake of a whole and healthy church. Here are a few random scenarios:

1. A leader with a strong prophetic anointing may not be at all fazed by strong prophetic people, welcoming and listening to them. The challenge comes when a prophet turns up with a higher level of gifting. Including such a prophet on team will be a test of unity when sparks fly, until the edgy stuff is sorted and the system functions well and the team settles down — what a relief!

2. Over time, radical leaders can become complacent and used to one another, tending to be suspicious or dismissive of new prophetic

sparks. Such a stuck-in-the-mud team can start to retard progress and growth. To safeguard against stagnation, and to remain open and flexible to new ideas from God, therefore, the next step is to ensure that there is an investment made into training and equipping the next generation of prophets. This might very well go against the grain, but it is critical to guarantee a malleable and flexible wineskin for the future. With fresh vision and visionaries at the helm the Church grows.

3. A leader who is not especially prophetic, but primarily pastoral and not easily threatened, may welcome and use prophets, even on team. This is a healthy reciprocal relationship where value and recognition is given and received from both sides. Each one sees the other as integral to the community and honours their position in Christ.

4. A less tolerant leader may find excuses to avoid prophetic people, unless they confirm and build up what the leader is doing or saying. And of course, that is a right role for a prophet to play: to be alongside a leader to encourage the leader's vision. The difficulty arises when a prophetic word is brought which challenges the direction or enlarges the vision, or even changes the vision. The leader is in a quandary and reluctant to engage with a word which alters his or her mindset. Usually sparks fly, the flames are dampened and the word dies out. If it was a true word, it was extinguished. We are commanded

not to quench the Spirit or despise the words of prophets, but to test everything and to hold fast to what is good (1 Thess 5:20–21).

5. A leader who takes the time to discern prophecy will find the investment well worth the effort, as mutual regard is built into the relationship. If a prophetic person gets it hopelessly wrong, but loving reassurance is part and parcel of any admonition, friendship is cultivated. Any leader who humbly receives a warning or vision, nurtures trust and respect. Any prophet who acts in love and not judgment will reap a harvest of doing good.

6. If there is little intentional weighing of prophetic words by leadership, or a long radio silence in response to prophecy, issues fester like sores in the body and are bound to crop up in destructive ways: hurt relationships; feelings of worthlessness and stupidity; anger and disappointment.

7. A leader who cherishes an 'open heaven' and sets a high value on freedom will see God present and at work everywhere, whenever people meet. This culture promotes an open door to prophecy and permission is given to deliver a revelation freely in small groups or in the main service—wherever, without any checks or balances. The downside is that the absence of any kind of discipline or built-in accountability can lead to weird teaching and a licence for anyone to say anything with gay abandon.

8. A leader who allows free reign will see prophecy set alight, not only in individuals but also in the congregation. Wise leadership will encourage this movement, making space for two or three to speak out in church gatherings and monitoring as appropriate.

9. A leader who feels that it's fine to be prophesying to one another in a small group 'over there', but is twitchy about letting people bring words in the main services 'over here', is clearly not thinking this through. To be unconcerned about what nonsense the body may be imparting liberally to one another out of earshot of leadership, and yet overly concerned about what is said in main meetings – when all are present to weigh and consider – makes no sense!

PROPHECY AND THE CHURCH

It would be easy to assume that prophecy is a one-off thing every now and then and that, having ironed out the flakiness, run-of-the-mill members of congregations are let off the hook. But Christians can never really rest on their laurels, summoned as they are, by the Lord, to *be* a prophetic community. If Christians are to show the world what Jesus Christ is like, then they are to *be* like him, *look* like him and bear testimony to his life. And when Christians do this together – live out his life as community – then they *are* the 'testimony of Jesus' and this witness *is* 'the Spirit of prophecy' (Rev. 19:10). Words and actions which prove the reality of Jesus Christ and are inhabited by the Holy Spirit are, in themselves, prophecy.

A retired businessman on a restorative justice Christian programme feels the impact of transformed lives as the love of Jesus touches and melts hardened criminal hearts to face the families of their victims.

Jesus said, 'I was in prison and you visited me' (Matt 25:26).

A Christian state prosecutor works closely with a prisoner, reaching out to him with compassionate justice. The leader of a notoriously dangerous national Mafia-type prison gang network, he is justly sentenced, but the dots are joined up in the valuable information gleaned and duly passed on to higher authorities in the prison system, by the very same Christian state prosecutor.

Jesus said, 'I was naked and you gave me clothing' (Matt 25:36). A very real and large part of witnessing to Jesus today is that, in the wake of so many disasters of epic proportions worldwide, or even smaller human tragedies, invariably we find a church opening its doors to the victims in the neighbourhood and working shoulder to shoulder alongside women and men of every faith, and with politicians and civic leaders, to bring practical assistance and the assurance of God in their midst.

We find, too, churches of different denominations, even poles apart doctrinally, joining hands in relief funding and expertise. And *this* cross-pollination is a vital and strategic prophetic sign of the oneness and unity for which Jesus prayed, and died.

Jesus said, 'I was a stranger and you welcomed me' (Matt 25:35):

A refugee from a war-torn country thousands of miles away arrived on the church's doorstep, sent by a policeman: That church will sort you out, he was told. Homeless, friendless and without food or clothing, the congregation enveloped the outcast with the loving kindness of the Lord and the necessities of life: a house, to which other refugees from his country soon flocked, work and English lessons, resulting in a book about his travels, *Walk this Way.*

A young woman arrived at the church, found her way to it. She turned out to have been in a neighbouring camp after the genocide, had walked the same way with her father. And they had been childhood sweethearts! Miracle of miracles!

A wedding, a celebration, two brand new lives. And the greater sign? During an away day looking at the person and work of the Holy Spirit, the young man was transported into the heavens. He flew, he said, over the world, to other nations. He met Jesus in that vision and his face shone with brightness ever after. Now his life was complete.

In obedience to Jesus' teaching of welcoming the stranger, the church community acted in his Spirit as his prophetic witness to a society which so easily turned away the orphan, widow and alien. To be a prophetic Church is to bring the light of kindness and compassion where all around is competitiveness and hardheartedness. To be a prophetic Church is to speak truth when lies predominate and compromise confounds. To be a prophetic church is to stay faithful to the testimony of Jesus, which is the Spirit of prophecy.

In the same way that the nation of Israel was chosen to be a living beacon to God among the nations, the Church of Christ is called to be a light to the world (see Ex 19:1-6). As living stones, our witness to Jesus Christ ought to be lively and adventurous, living as we do on the Devil's doorstep:

> But you are a chosen race, a royal priesthood, a holy nation, God's own people, in order that you may proclaim the mighty acts of him who called you out of darkness into his marvelous light.
> **1 Peter 2:9**

In the darkness, there is One who hears, One who listens, One who stoops down and bends His ear. Our tumults do reach Him. He is not immune, detached and incapable of suffering. He has already suffered: on the cross, in the person of Jesus Christ. Forever that pain, the world's pain, is in the very heart of God, nailed to Him.

Today, in our times, he is willing to come down to our aid and he does though his Body on earth. We are Jesus' hands and feet, Jesus' eyes and ears, Jesus' very life. He tells us what to do, when to do it and how to do it. He speaks his prophetic word and we are healed, and we go on our way to do his will and to make a difference in our times, in our countries, workplaces, families and neighbourhoods.

QUESTIONS FOR FURTHER DISCUSSION

Does your church or organisation make it easy for prophecies to be delivered and heard? If not, what is the remedy and how could communication be improved?

Do you recognise any of the reactions regarding prophets in yourself, as an ordinary member of a congregation, or as a leader?

In what ways is your church or organisation or network a prophetic beacon in the community or nation?

Prophecy for Anyone

A FINAL WORD

Like those first disciples, handling twelve baskets of leftover fragments from the bread and fish meal which fed five thousand (not counting children and women), hopefully the reader of this material has gathered a small fragment as a take home basket. Whatever the morsel or morsels, the prayer behind this book is that it would uplift and inspire and challenge people onwards and upwards in their Christian journey. And as the offering of the small boy, by prayer, was multiplied, so may this nugget of insight or revelation become much in the hands of the Father, and become a key to unlock the doors which hitherto have been firmly barred to our entreaties.

For prophetic vision, that which grows the Church, when accompanied by, bathed and immersed in, love, is an unstoppable force for mission. Without heavenly vision, we are less than, far less than, the giants of faith we are called to be. We are told that, 'Where there is no vision the people perish' (Jer 29:18, KJV). Therefore, we are instructed: 'Today, if you hear his voice, do not harden your hearts' (Heb 4:7).

And all this, all this attentiveness to the voice of the Shepherd, can get our goat, can be leverage for anger, or indignation—or change. For prophecy is God's agent of change, and prophets are his change agents. To enter the regions of prophecy is to surrender to all the surprises of unfamiliar ground. How then shall we tread: with suspicion, or with awe and excitement?